Ranger Rick's NatureScope

AMAZING MAMMALS, PART I

National Wildlife Federation

Chelsea House Publishers
Philadelphia

This Chelsea House edition of NatureScope® with permission of Learning Triangle Press, an imprint of McGraw-Hill.

First published in hardback edition ©1999 Chelsea House Publishers.

Library of Congress Cataloging-in-Publication Data

Amazing mammals / National Wildlife Federation.
   p. cm. — (Ranger Rick's naturescope)
   Originally published: New York: Learning Triangle Press, c 1998.
   Includes bibliographical references and index.
   ISBN 0-7910-4878-0 (pt. 1) — ISBN 0-7910-4879-9 (pt. 2)
   1. Mammals—Study and teaching (Elementary)—Activity programs.
   I. National Wildlife Federation. II. Series.
   [Ql706.4.A535 1998]
   372.3'57—dc21
                             98-39958
                                   CIP

NatureScope® was originally conceived by National Wildlife Federation's School Programs Editorial Staff, under the direction of Judy Braus, Editor. Special thanks to all of the Editorial Staff, Scientific, Educational Consultants and Contributors who brought this series of eighteen publications to life.

Other Titles in Ranger Rick's NatureScope

TABLE OF CONTENTS

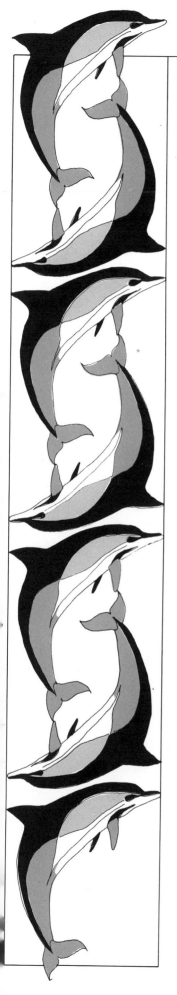

A Close-Up Look At Amazing Mammals

ooking at the Table of Contents, you can see we've divided *Amazing Mammals* into four chapters (each of which deals with a broad mammal theme) and a craft section. Each of the four chapters includes *background information* that explains concepts and vocabulary, *activities* that relate to the chapter theme, and *Copycat Pages* that reinforce many of the concepts introduced in the activities.

You can choose single activity ideas or teach each chapter as a unit. Either way, each activity stands by itself and includes teaching objectives, a list of materials needed, suggested age groups, subjects covered, and a step-by-step explanation of how to do the activity. (The objectives, materials, age groups, and subjects are highlighted in the left-hand margin for easy reference.)

AGE GROUPS

The suggested age groups are:
- Primary (grades K–2)
- Intermediate (grades 3–5)
- Advanced (grades 6–7)

Each chapter begins with primary activities and ends with intermediate or advanced activities. But don't feel bound by the grade levels we suggest. Resourceful teachers, naturalists, parents, and club leaders can adapt most of these activities to fit their particular age group and needs.

OUTDOOR ACTIVITIES

No matter where you live there are many mammal-related activities you can do outside. We've included several outdoor activities in this issue. These are coded in the chapters in which they appear with this symbol:

COPYCAT PAGES

The *Copycat Pages* supplement the activities and include ready-to-copy games, puzzles, coloring pages, and worksheets. *Answers to all Copycat Pages are in the texts of the activities.*

WHAT'S AT THE END

The fifth section, *Crafty Corner,* will give you some art and craft ideas that complement many of the activities in the first four sections. *Applying You Knowledge* and the Bibliography are loaded with the reference suggestions that include books, films, and mammal posters. It also has mammal questions and answers, a mammal glossary, and suggestions for where to get more mamma information.

WHAT MAKES A MAMMAL A MAMMAL?

What do you have in common with a pint-sized bat? A lot! Both of you are mammals. And all mammals, from humans to bats to bears, share many characteristics. In this chapter we'll look at the many ways mammals are alike, as well as some of the ways they're different. We'll also compare mammals with other animal groups and travel back about 200 million years to see how mammals got their start.

MAMMALS INSIDE AND OUT

Backbones and Braincases: Mammals belong to a group of animals called vertebrates. They make up one group (*class*) of vertebrates called *Mammalia*. Fish, amphibians, reptiles, and birds are the other classes of vertebrates.

Like most vertebrates, mammals have a bony backbone called a vertebral column. (Instead of bone, sharks and some other primitive fish have support systems made of a softer material called cartilage.) And like all vertebrates, they have a *cranium*—a hard case made of bone or cartilage that surrounds the brain.

Active and Warm-blooded: Mammals and birds are the only two animal groups that are warm-blooded. That means their body temperatures remain about the same all the time, even if the temperature around them changes. Unlike cold-blooded animals, warm-blooded animals can be active in a wide range of temperatures. But warm-blooded animals burn a lot more fuel than cold-blooded vertebrates do, and that's why mammals and birds eat more than reptiles, amphibians, and fish do.

Marvelous Milk: Unlike all other animals, female mammals nurse their young with milk that's produced in glands inside their bodies. Most mammal babies suck the milk from their mothers' nipples. But some mammals, such as platypuses, don't have nipples. Instead, their milk oozes out of glands on their bellies, where the young suck it up.

Skin and Glands: Mammal skin not only protects a mammal, it also produces special structures such as hair, claws, nails, hooves, horns, and pads. Mammals such as elephants and rhinos have a very thick outer layer of skin. But some mammals, especially those covered with fur, have very thin and soft skin.

Mammal skin is also loaded with different kinds of glands: mammary, oil, sweat, and scent glands. Mammary glands produce milk that female mammals use to nurse their young. Oil glands produce oil that helps lubricate the hair and skin and in some mammals helps waterproof the fur. Sweat glands produce sweat (a mixture of salts and water), which helps mammals cool off as it evaporates from their skin. And scent glands produce substances that mammals use for communication. In a few mammals, such as skunks, some of the scent glands are used for defense. *Note:* All mammals have mammary glands, but not all mammals have oil, sweat, or scent glands.

(continued next page)

Hairy Beasts: Hair is something you won't find on anything but a mammal. (Other animals, such as some insects and birds, have hairlike structures. But only mammals have true hair.) Although most mammals have some type of hair, the form varies from species to species. For example, many mammals, such as cats and bears, have thick *fur* covering most of their bodies. The fur acts like a winter coat—holding in heat and keeping out cold. Other mammals—specifically, some of the whales—have only a few coarse hairs on their chins and snouts. And most other whales and dolphins, unlike all other mammals, don't have any hair at all.

Hair does more than keep mammals warm. For example, the quills on a porcupine and the spines on a hedgehog are modified hairs that provide protection against enemies. Many mammals also have special types of hair around their eyes, nose, and ears that help keep out dust, insects, and other foreign objects. And eyebrows decrease the amount of light that is reflected into a mammal's eyes. Many mammals also have special sensory hairs, called *whiskers* or *vibrissae,* on their cheeks, lips, and other parts of the head. Whiskers help an animal feel its way around—especially in the dark. (For more about hair, see "The Layered Wolf" on page 11.)

An Inside Look: Mammals have a very efficient metabolism. Their blood cells, pumped through a powerful, four-chambered heart, can carry more oxygen than the blood cells of any other type of animal. This efficient blood transport system is very important to mammals and allows them to be more active than reptiles, fish, and other cold-blooded animals.

Mammals also have a very efficient way of breathing. They're the only animals with a *diaphragm*—a muscle in the chest that expands the chest cavity with each breath, separating the chest from the abdomen and allowing more air to enter the lungs.

A Bigger and Better Brain: The *central nervous system* in mammals—the brain and spinal cord—is amazing. As in other types of animals, it regulates most of what the body does. But in mammals, it is more complex and advanced than in any other animal group. (For more about the mammal brain, see "The Layered Wolf" on page 12.)

Snip, Grind, and Stab: Almost all mammals have teeth. But the type, arrangement, and number of teeth vary from species to species. And unlike other vertebrates, mammals have specialized teeth for eating different kinds of foods.

There are three basic kinds of mammal teeth: *incisors,* or front teeth; *canines,* or eye teeth; and *premolars* and *molars,* or cheek teeth. You can usually tell what a mammal eats by looking at the type of teeth it has. For example, some grazers, such as kangaroos, have a few incisors on their lower and upper jaws for snipping grass. They also have large, flat, grinding molars for chewing the grass once it's in their mouths. But kangaroos don't have any canines. On the other hand, meat eaters, such as foxes and wolves, have very large, sharp canines for stabbing and holding prey. They also have strong cheek teeth that can crush bone and cut flesh. (For more about the different types of food mammals eat, see page 35.)

MAKING SENSE OF THE SENSES

Great Sniffers: Without a good nose, many mammals would have a difficult time finding food, a mate, or a place to live—and they'd also have a hard time detecting enemies. For many mammals, smell is the most important sense. (We humans, as well as a few monkeys and apes, have a relatively poor sense of smell. And dolphins and whales don't seem to have any sense of smell.)

Many species also depend on certain scents to communicate with other

jaguar

Leonard Lee Rue III

mammals. For example, dogs and cats mark their territories with urine and other substances, and wildebeests stake out territories using scent from special glands on their feet.

We're All Ears: Unlike other types of animals, most mammals have outer ears to help catch sound waves and funnel them into the middle and inner ears. And most mammals have an extraordinary sense of hearing and can pick up sounds that most other animals (including some mammals) can't hear. For example, many mice communicate with sounds that are about five times higher in pitch than humans can hear.

Bright Eyes: Humans, apes, and other primates hold the record for the best mammal eyesight during the day. (Some birds are the only vertebrates that have better vision than primates.) And unlike those of many mammals, the eyes of primates face forward. This allows them to focus on the same object with both eyes, giving them a good depth of field—important for judging distances. (This type of sight is called *binocular vision.*) Primates also have the ability to see color, unlike many other types of mammals.

Most mammals that are active at night have a special reflective layer in their eyes that helps them see better in the dark. This layer reflects more light to the retina and is what causes *eyeshine*—the glow you see when you shine a light into the eyes of a cat, raccoon, or other nocturnal mammal. Mammals that spend a lot of time burrowing in the ground, such as moles, often have poor eyesight or are almost blind.

MAMMALS THROUGH TIME

An Ancient Beginning: Mammals are some of the youngest animals around, in terms of their evolutionary history. The first mammals evolved from mammal-like reptiles that lived about 200 million years ago. These mammal-like reptiles had some reptilian characteristics, but they also had many mammalian characteristics, such as mammal-like teeth, skulls, and limbs.

It was during the days of the dinosaurs that the first true mammals—small, shrewlike creatures—first appeared. These first mammals lived in the shadow of the dominant dinosaurs, scurrying about in the undergrowth in search of insects and worms. And unlike most of the huge reptiles, these primitive mammals were probably active at night.

When the Dinosaurs Disappeared: For some reason, the dinosaurs and many other types of animals and plants that lived about 65 million years ago became extinct. No one knows exactly why these animals and plants died. But it gave the mammals that survived a chance to branch out and "take over." And it wasn't long before the Age of Mammals—an age that we are still living in today—took off.

Changing Through Time: Over millions and millions of years, mammals have changed in many ways. For example, seals today evolved long ago from land animals that had legs. And at one time, the ancestors of bats could not fly. But some mammals, such as opossums, have changed hardly at all since they first evolved—and they are still able to survive today.

Putting Order to the Mammals: Today there are over 4000 species of mammals, divided into about twenty different groups, or *orders.* (Not all mammalogists agree on exactly how many orders there should be.) If you could line up all 4000 species, side by side, you'd see an incredible assortment of creatures. But no matter how different they look—the runners, the hoppers, the swimmers, the fliers, the crawlers, and the walkers—all of them evolved from those tiny shrewlike creatures that lived 200 million years ago.

For the Record

Run, jump, and take some measurements to see how humans compare with other mammals.

___

Objectives:
Compare mammal sizes and skills. Describe three mammal record holders.

Ages:
Primary and Intermediate

Materials:
- *copies of page 19*
- *materials for the contest events (see "Can You Beat the Best?" on page 7)*

Subjects:
Science and Physical Education

I n this activity the kids in your group will learn about some neat mammal statistics and get a feeling for how diverse mammals are. Then they can compete in a contest and compare their own sizes and abilities with those of other mammals.

Begin by telling the kids that mammals come in all sizes and shapes and with all kinds of natural abilities that help them survive. Then pass out copies of page 19 and use the following information to talk about the mammals on the sheet.

THE FASTEST MAMMALS

Cheetah: Fastest land mammal over a short distance. May run at speeds of over 60 miles (100 km) per hour for 200-300 yards (180-270 m). Its explosive speed helps it catch its prey.

Pronghorn: Fastest land mammal over a long distance. Can easily run 35-45 miles (55-70 km) per hour for 4 miles (6 km) and can reach speeds of 55 miles (90 km) per hour for shorter distances. Being able to run fast for long periods of time helps pronghorns outrun their predators.

Killer Whale: Fastest marine mammal over a short distance. Can sometimes swim at speeds of up to 35 miles (55 km) per hour for about 500 yards (450 m). Killer whales prey on fish, squid, and marine mammals such as seals and other whales.

THE LARGEST MAMMALS

Blue Whale: Largest animal in the world. Also the largest animal that's ever lived. May grow to more than 100 feet (30 m) long and weigh more than 150 tons (135 t). Blue whales feed on tiny shrimplike animals called *krill*.

Giraffe: Tallest land mammal—19 feet (6 m) high. Giraffes' long necks help them reach leaves and other food high in the treetops.

African Elephant: Largest land animal. This elephant may stand more than 10½ feet (3.2 m) tall at the shoulder and weigh more than 6½ tons (6 t). Elephants have large, thick legs that support their massive weight.

Indricotherium (in-DRICK-uh-THIH-ree-um): Largest land mammal ever to exist. It was 35 to 37 feet (10.5-11 m) long and stood about 18 feet (5 m) tall at the shoulder. Indricotheriums lived 37-15 million years ago, at the same time as the earliest camels, squirrels, and dogs. (Also known as *Baluchitherium*.)

SOME OF THE BEST JUMPERS

Red Kangaroo: Can jump more than 40 feet (12 m) in one bound and can jump more than 10 feet (3 m) high. Kangaroos escape predators by bounding away from them in a series of zigzag jumps.

Jerboa: Can broad jump up to 10 feet (3 m) in a single bound. (Jerboas' bodies may be only 5 inches [12.5 cm] long!) Like kangaroos, jerboas escape predators by jumping away in a zigzag pattern. (Live in arid areas from the Sahara Desert across southwestern and central Asia to the Gobi Desert.)

Cougar: Can jump 18 feet (5 m) high and can broad jump 30 feet (9 m). A cougar stalks its prey, then often leaps onto the animal's back.

Sperm Whale: Can hold its breath for one hour and 15 minutes. Sperm whales get a lot of their food from the sea floor and may have to dive down more than 3000 feet (900 m) to reach bottom.

Weddell (WED-ul) Seal: Can hold its breath for up to one hour. These Antarctic seals spend a lot of time under the ice and often have to chew through it in order to breathe.

CAN YOU BEAT THE BEST?

After your discussion, ask the kids how well they think they'd compare with any of the animals on page 19. Then tell them that they're going to compete in a contest to find out exactly how they do compare with these other mammals. Here are some ideas for the "events" in your contest:

- **25-yard (23-m) Dash:** Compare the fastest kid with a cheetah. (A cheetah could run the race in less than one second!) *Note:* This figure represents a cheetah's top speed and was not measured from a standing-still starting position. To make the comparison a little more realistic, you may want to have the kids run a 50-yard (45-m) dash, timing them from yard 25 to the end.
- **100-yard (90-m) Dash:** Compare the fastest kid with a cheetah and a pronghorn. (Both a cheetah and a pronghorn could finish the race in about 3½ seconds. And a pronghorn could run the race four times in a row in only 15 seconds! [See note above. You may want to have the kids run a 125-yard (113-m) dash, timing them from yard 25 to the end.])
- **50-yard (46-m) Swimming Race:** Compare the fastest kid with a killer whale. (A killer whale could swim the race in about 3 seconds.)
- **40-foot (12-m) Hop:** Measure off a 40-foot (12-m) distance and see who can jump from one end to the other in the least number of hops. Compare this number with that of a kangaroo. (A red kangaroo could jump the distance in one hop!)

- **Broad Jump:** Compare the longest jump with those of a cougar and a jerboa. (A cougar could jump 30 feet [9 m] in a single jump and a tiny jerboa could jump 10 feet [3 m]!)
- **High Jump:** Make a chalk mark 5 feet (1.5 m) high on an outside wall. Then let the kids try to jump so their feet are even with the mark. (Don't let them take any steps before they jump.) Compare the kids' attempts with those of a kangaroo and a cougar. (A red kangaroo could jump almost twice as high as the mark and a cougar could easily jump three times higher!)
- **How Long?:** Measure off a 100-foot (30-m) distance and see how many kids it takes to fill up the distance if they lie down on the ground head-to-toe. Compare this number with the length of a blue whale. (One blue whale could fill the entire distance.)
- **Tipping the Scales:** Weigh everybody in your group and then have the kids figure out how many of them it would take to tip the scales on an elephant. (An African elephant can weigh up to 6½ tons [6 t].)
- **The Great Breath Hold:** Have the kids try to hold their breath for as long as they comfortably can. Compare their abilities with those of a Weddell seal and a sperm whale. (A Weddell seal can hold its breath for an hour and a sperm whale can hold its breath for *more* than that.)

Safety Note: Warn the children not to try to hold their breath for too long.

Nose Know-How

Objectives:
Explain how a mammal's sense of smell works. Describe some ways that smell is important to mammals.

Ages:
Primary, Intermediate, and Advanced

Materials:
- *several different scents (vanilla, peppermint, lemon, maple, and so on)*
- *empty film canisters*
- *cotton balls*
- *paper and pencils*
- *yarn*
- *markers*
- *reference books*
- *masking tape*
- *cardboard*
- *rubber bands*
- *paper punch*
- *stockings (optional)*

Subject:
Science

Smell is the most important sense for most mammals. They use their noses to detect predators or prey, to distinguish between family and non-family members, to find mates, and to recognize their territories and those of other mammals. In this activity the kids in your group can put their own noses to "work" to learn how and why a sense of smell is important to mammals.

Begin by discussing how a mammal's sense of smell works. Tell the kids that deep inside a mammal's nose is an area called the *olfactory (ol-FAC-tor-ee) region*. And the olfactory region has lots of "smelling" nerves. When people or other mammals breathe air through their noses, odors in the air "turn on" these special smelling nerves. Biologists aren't exactly sure how the brain identifies the different odors, but they do know that mammals can distinguish among thousands of different ones.

An odor isn't always easy to smell and identify. Sometimes odors are very faint and mammals must sniff (get more air into the olfactory region) to get a better idea of what an odor is and where it's coming

from. Some mammals also snort to clear all of the "old" air out of their noses so they can get a better whiff of a new odor.

Next discuss the specific ways mammals use their sense of smell. Tell the kids that mammals may use their sense of smell to detect predators, smell food, and taste food. But smell is also important for many other reasons. For example, most male mammals can tell if a female is ready to mate by detecting a certain odor she gives off (dogs, horses, wildebeests). And many mammals mark their territories with urine or feces (wolves, cats, dogs, rhinos, most primates) and special scents from anal glands (beavers, hyenas) or glands in their feet (wildebeests) or other parts of their bodies.

Smell also helps some mammal family members recognize each other. When most mammals meet they identify each other by sniffing. And many mother mammals learn to recognize the sight, taste, and smell of their young as soon as they're born.

Now give the kids a chance to "work" their own noses. Here are a few ideas that you can try:

Luise Woelflein

THE NOSE KNOWS

Before you get started with this activity, make ten different scent containers using empty film canisters and cotton balls. First soak each cotton ball in a different flavoring or scent (such as lemon, orange, maple, vanilla, coconut, root beer, chocolate, cinnamon, peppermint, and so on) and put each one in a different canister. (You can also use chocolate chips, orange peel, pine needles, and other fragrant items—but cover them with a cotton ball so the kids can't see them.) Then number each canister on the bottom and top with masking tape and a marker. (These numbers will be used in "Keeping Track of Baby," on the next page.)

Tell the kids that they're going to get a chance to see how well they can recognize

different odors. First have them sit in a big circle. Then pass each canister around one at a time. Tell the kids not to let anyone else know what they think each smell is. After everyone has had a chance to smell what's in a particular canister, talk about what the odor was before passing around the next canister.

To wrap up the activity, discuss how a good sense of smell is important to mammals. Explain that most mammals, including people, are able to identify thousands of different odors. Ask the kids what could happen if a wild mammal failed to recognize a particular odor. (It could become a predator's dinner, lose its chance to catch a meal, mistake an intruder for a relative, eat food that is rotten enough to make it ill, and so on.)

KEEPING TRACK OF BABY

Divide the group into two teams. Tell one team they are mammal mothers and tell the other they are mammal babies. Explain that each species of mammal has a scent that is different from those of all other mammals. Also tell them that each mammal mother instinctively knows its baby's scent.

Now have the "mothers" stand at the front of the room and the "babies" stand at the far end of the room. Give each of the mothers a film canister with a scent in it. (See "The Nose Knows," on page 8.) For a group of 30 children, you will need 15 different scents. Tell the mothers to try to memorize their particular scents. Then have them take the caps off their canisters and hold onto them while you collect the bottoms, mix them up, and give one to each baby. Explain that each mother must now try to find the right baby by sniffing the canisters and finding the correct scent. (Have the kids of the "baby" team stand still, holding their canisters out for the mothers to sniff.) You can have each mother take a turn, one at a time, or have all the mothers sniff out their babies at the same time. After all the mothers find their babies, have everyone check to make sure their numbers match. Then switch roles and play again.

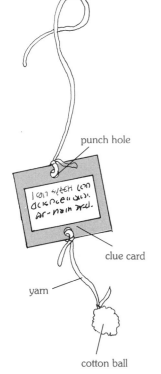

punch hole

clue card

yarn

cotton ball

SNIFFING OUT A TRAIL

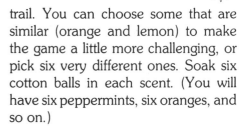

In this sniffing game, your kids will get a chance to follow a scent trail to find mammal clues. Here's what to do:

Setting Up the Trail

1. Cut out 30 sturdy cardboard squares—5 × 5″ (12 x 12 cm)—and 60 eight-inch (20-cm) strands of yarn. Punch a hole in the top and bottom center of each card (see diagram).

2. Tie a piece of yarn through each hole and copy each of the clues listed at the end of this activity on a separate card. (We've set this up so that there will be five clue cards for each mammal, but you may need to adjust the number of clue cards to fit the number of kids in your group.)

3. Pick six scents to use for the sniffing trail. You can choose some that are similar (orange and lemon) to make the game a little more challenging, or pick six very different ones. Soak six cotton balls in each scent. (You will have six peppermints, six oranges, and so on.)

4. Tie each cotton ball of the same scent to the five clue cards for that mammal. (For example, all the moose clues could have cotton balls that are soaked with peppermint. The sixth cotton ball of each scent will be used as a "sample" scent later.)

Note: If you use scents that turn the cotton balls different colors (for example, maple flavoring makes a cotton ball brown and strawberry makes a cotton ball pink), cover each cotton ball with a tiny piece of stocking to keep the kids from keying in on color. (You can just staple it around each of the 36 cotton balls.)

Now set up the trail outside. Choose a path that the kids can easily follow (a nature trail, a path around the schoolyard or building, and so on) and pick five stations along that path. At station 1, hang the habitat clues; at station 2, hang the food clues; at station 3, hang the description clues; at station 4, hang the reproduction clues; and at station 5, hang the special facts clues. *(continued next page)*

Luise Woelflein

How to Play

Divide the group into six teams and explain that each team represents a different type of female mammal. To discover which mammal they are, the members of each team will have to follow the correct scent trail, copy down the clues along the way, and then figure out which mammal fits all the clues.

Give each person a pencil and a pad of paper or have him or her make a clipboard by fastening a piece of paper to a piece of cardboard with a rubber band. Then give each team a different scent. (Have them smell the sixth cotton ball soaked in their scent.) Tell them they will need to memorize their scent in order to figure out what mammal they are.

Then take them outside and show them the trail. Explain that one person from each team will start at each station. All the team members must sniff all the cotton balls at their respective stations until they find the one that matches their scent. When they find the right scent, they should write down the clue that appears on the card the scent is attached to.

Each person must visit all five stations in order to get all five clues. After all team members have visited all five stations, have them regroup and try to figure out which mammal they are. Then go over all the clues with the entire group.

MOOSE

Description:
I am a large, hooved mammal with a blackish-brown coat. The hair that hangs from my mate's throat looks like a bell. His antlers are very large.
Habitat:
I live in marshy forests in the northern United States, and in parts of Canada, northern Europe, and other northern areas.
Food:
I eat tree leaves and water plants.
Reproduction:
My gestation period is 8 months. I have 1 to 2 young at a time.
Special Facts:
I can swim long distances. Wolves are my main predators.

RACCOON

Description:
I have a plump body with a grayish coat.
Habitat:
I live in woodlands and like to hang around streams, ponds, and lakes. I'm found in most parts of the United States and in parts of South America and Canada. (I sometimes visit people's backyards.)
Food:
I eat small fish, crayfish, frogs, eggs, mice, fruits, nuts, and some plants.
Reproduction:
My gestation period is a little over 2 months. I have 3 to 6 young at a time.
Special Facts:
Some people say I wash my food before I eat it, but I really don't.

GRAY SQUIRREL

Description:
I have a gray coat and a fuzzy tail.
Habitat:
I live just about anywhere there are deciduous trees—even in cities.
Food:
I eat mostly nuts and fruits, although sometimes I'll eat insects, small birds, and eggs.
Reproduction:
My gestation period is 6 weeks. I can have as many as 9 young at a time.
Special Facts:
I often build a leafy nest in the treetops.

CHIMPANZEE

Description:
My coat is black, but it starts to turn gray as I get older.
Habitat:
I usually live in humid forests in Africa. But sometimes you can see me on dry savannahs.
Food:
I eat mostly plants, but my diet can also include termites and small mammals.
Reproduction:
My gestation period is 7 to 8 months. I usually have only 1 baby at a time.
Special Facts:
I'm a good climber and usually sleep in trees.

GRAY WOLF

Description:
The color of my coat ranges from white to gray to black.
Habitat:
You can find me in parts of North America, Europe, and Asia. I live in forests, on mountains, and in deserts.
Food:
I eat large mammals such as moose, deer, and caribou. I also eat smaller mammals such as beavers and hares.
Reproduction:
My gestation period is 2 months. I usually have 4 to 7 babies at a time.
Special Facts:
I am related to dogs. Most of the time I live in a family pack.

LION

Description:
My coat is yellowish-brown. I have powerful jaws.
Habitat:
I live in the grasslands and deserts of Africa.
Food:
I eat large prey such as zebras and antelopes. I also eat smaller animals such as hares and birds.
Reproduction:
My gestation period is 3 to 4 months. I usually have 1 to 5 young at a time.
Special Facts:
We females do most of the hunting for our family group.

The Layered Wolf

Take a look at mammal characteristics by making a "layered wolf."

Objectives:
Describe the main characteristics of a mammal. Name some of the features of a wolf and describe how they help it survive.

Ages:
Intermediate

Materials:
- *copies of page 20*
- *tracing paper*
- *glue*
- *construction paper*
- *scissors*
- *crayons or markers*
- *manilla folders or thin cardboard*
- *picture of a gray wolf*
- *stapler*
- *chalkboard or easel paper (optional)*

Subjects:
Science and Art

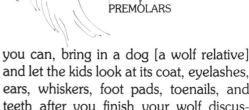

In this activity the kids in your group can take a close-up look at mammal characteristics by making their own "layered wolves." But before the kids start on their wolves, make one yourself to use in a discussion about mammal characteristics. (See the instructions at the end of this activity.) Here's a look at some of the things to point out in your discussion. (If you can, bring in a dog [a wolf relative] and let the kids look at its coat, eyelashes, ears, whiskers, foot pads, toenails, and teeth after you finish your wolf discussion.)

DECORATED SHEET: HAIR

Begin by explaining that hair helps keep many mammals warm. Point to the hair on your wolf and explain that gray wolves have a double layer of hair just as many other mammals do. The *underfur,* which is closest to the wolf's body, is dense and woolly and insulates the animal. The outer layer, or *guard hair,* is rough and keeps the wolf dry by shedding moisture. (Oil coats the guard hair, which makes water roll off instead of letting it soak in. See "Undecorated Sheet: Skin, Nose, and Ears" for information about oil glands in mammal skin.) The guard hair also gives a smooth, sleek shape to the wolf's coat.

A gray wolf's outer layer of hair is made of different colored hairs. Because of this, gray wolves may look black, white, reddish, yellowish, tan, gray, silver, or brown.

Next point to the whiskers on the wolf's face. Explain that these hairs are very sensitive. They help the wolf feel around when it's sniffing a trail, walking through brush, going through small spaces, and so on. You can also point out that the wolf's eyelashes help keep dust and other things out of its eyes, just as our own eyelashes do.

UNDECORATED SHEET: SKIN, NOSE, AND EARS

Tell the kids that all mammals' hair is produced in their skin and so are their horns, hooves, and nails. Point to the paw that you traced and explain that the wolf's blunt claws and spongy, calloused pads are produced in its skin. These claws and pads help the wolf walk and run, and give it a good grip on ice, snow, and other surfaces.

Then explain that mammal skin is also full of nerves that respond to touch. These nerves are usually all over mammals' bodies. But some mammals have special body parts such as whiskers, tails, paws,

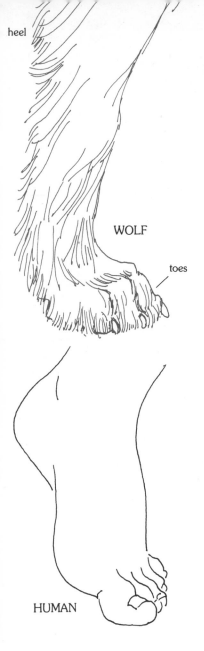

heel

WOLF

toes

HUMAN

or fingers which are supersensitive to touch.

Next tell the kids that mammal skin often has all kinds of glands in it too. Explain that the wolf's oil glands help keep moisture from soaking into its coat and reaching the skin. And the mammary glands produce milk that the female uses to feed her young. (The young suckle milk from nipples, or *mammae*. Different mammal species have different numbers of mammae. For example, female wolves have ten.) *Note:* Only a female with pups has visible mammae. The mammae show for about a month.

Many mammals also have scent glands in their skin. Point to the pads on the wolf's paw and explain that when a wolf scratches the ground with its feet it releases odors from scent glands between these pads. This scent helps the wolf mark its territory. (The main way a wolf marks its territory, though, is with urine and, to a lesser extent, feces. Wolves leave urine and feces on lots of prominent places [stumps, rocks, snowbanks] throughout their territories.) Wolves also have anal glands that give their droppings a special scent.

Now point to the wolf's snout and ex-

plain that smell is one of the most important senses for wolves. Wolves use their noses to recognize their own territorial markings and the territorial markings of other wolves. They also use them to identify pack members and to locate prey. Then tell the kids that, inside a wolf's long snout, there are lots of olfactory nerve endings that give the animal a very keen sense of smell. A wolf can smell prey that's over a mile (1.6 km) away!

Finally, point to the wolf's ears and explain that mammals are the only animals with outer ears. Other animals have simple openings leading to their eardrums. Often these openings aren't visible. (For example, a bird's ears are covered by its feathers.)

The outer ears of some mammals have different functions. For example, the shape of some bats' ears help them gather sound—a helpful adaptation for hunting insects with echolocation. Other mammals' ears, such as those of jackrabbits and other desert dwellers, are loaded with blood vessels that help them get rid of excess heat. (See page 27 of *NatureScope—Discovering Deserts* [Vol. 1, No. 5] for more about how a desert mammal's ears keep it from overheating.)

INSIDE THE WOLF

Use the diagrams shown below, your copy of page 20, and the following information to talk about a mammal's "insides":

- **Backbone**—This protects a vertebrate's spinal cord and gives the animal support. All mammals have backbones.

THE FINISHED WOLF

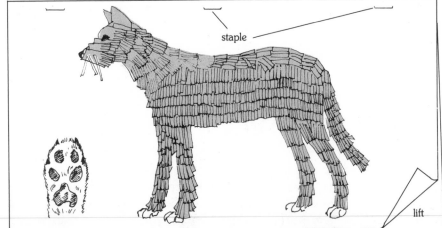

staple

lift

- **Heart**—Like all mammals, wolves have powerful, four-chambered hearts. And like all mammals, their blood transport system is very efficient. (See "An Inside Look" on page 4.)
- **Lungs**—A strong muscle called the diaphragm, found only in mammals, helps get air into the lungs and makes breathing more efficient. (See "An Inside Look" on page 4.)
- **Brain**—A mammal's central nervous system is very complex and advanced. Most mammal brains are larger than the brains of other, similar-sized animals. And mammals have a more developed *cerebral cortex*—the part of the brain where learning takes place. Because they have an advanced ability to learn, mammals are better able to store important information that they can use later.
- **Teeth**—Type, arrangement, and

number varies from mammal to mammal. Wolves are carnivores (meat eaters) and their large teeth are highly specialized. Use the diagram on page 11 (you might want to copy a simplified version on a chalkboard or large piece of easel paper) along with the following information to talk about a wolf's teeth:

Wolves use their long canine teeth to grab and kill their prey. With their short incisors they nibble and tear food, and with their sharp premolars they chew their food. Their flat molars can crush bone. An adult wolf's jaw has incredible power—it can slice through frozen meat and crush some bones.

- **Feet**—Mammals have all kinds of ways of getting around—from walking to swimming to flying. And mammals that walk (or run) from place to place may do so on the soles of their feet, on their toes, or on their nails. Wolves walk on their toes. (You can show the kids the diagram on page 12. For more about how mammals get around see "Mammals on the Move" on page 38.)

How To Make A Layered Wolf

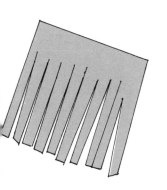

For group leaders only: Put an 8½ × 11-inch sheet of tracing paper over page 20 and trace the wolf's paw and the outline of the wolf's body. (*Do not* trace the brain, bones, heart, lungs, and diaphragm.) Then photocopy your tracing so that you have two copies for yourself plus one copy for each child in the group. You will be decorating one of your copies to use when discussing mammal hair (see step 1, below, and the section titled "Decorated Sheet: Hair") and you'll be using the other copy when discussing mammal skin (see the section titled "Undecorated Sheet: Skin, Nose, and Ears"). The kids will use their copies for step 1 in the following directions.

1. Glue the copy of the tracing to a thin piece of cardboard or a manilla folder. Then give the wolf its hair by gluing strips of fringed construction paper onto it (see diagram). (You might want to glue down an extra layer for under-fur.) Be sure to add whiskers and eyelashes! (Show the kids pictures of a gray wolf and encourage them to decorate their wolves as accurately as possible.)

2. Color page 20 and glue it to a piece of thin cardboard. (*Group leaders:* You might want to color only the diaphragm, backbone, heart, lungs, brain, and teeth so they'll stand out when you use the sheet in your discussion.) Then put the decorated sheet on top of this colored sheet. (*Group leaders:* Put the decorated sheet on top of the undecorated sheet, then put both of these on top of the colored sheet.)

3. Staple all of the sheets together across the top.

The kids can lift up the the outer layer to see what's inside the wolf's body.

The Vertebrate Grab Game

Discuss the characteristics of the five major vertebrate groups, then play a running game.

Objectives:
Define vertebrate. *Describe four characteristics that make a mammal a mammal. Describe several characteristics of two other kinds of vertebrates.*
(continued next page)

All mammals are vertebrates (animals with backbones). And birds, amphibians, fish, and reptiles are vertebrates too. In this activity the kids in your group will discover what makes mammals different from other vertebrates as they learn about the characteristics of the five major vertebrate groups.

Before you get started, copy each of the generalized body forms (drawn in the margin on the next page) onto a piece of cardboard. Then cut out each figure and label it mammal, bird, amphibian, fish, or reptile.

Now pass out copies of page 21 to the kids. Explain that birds, reptiles, fish, amphibians, and mammals are all vertebrates (animals with backbones) but that each group of vertebrates is very different from the others. The general characteristics of all five groups are listed on page 21. Have the kids read along on their sheets as you discuss each group using the background information on pages 3-5 and the following information:

Ages:
Intermediate

Materials:
- *copies of page 21*
- *cardboard*
- *scissors*
- *copy of the clues provided in the activity*
- *paper and pencil*

Subject:
Science

AMPHIBIAN

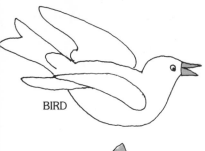

BIRD

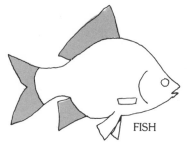

FISH

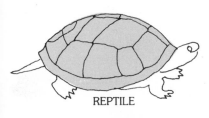

REPTILE

MAMMAL

AMPHIBIANS

Amphibians have no hair, feathers, or scales. Instead, many of these cold-blooded vertebrates have smooth skin that's kept moist by a slimy substance called *mucus*. (Toads are an exception. They have thick, leathery skin.) Most amphibians lay their eggs in water, but some lay them in moist places on land. The young pass through a larval stage, usually in water, before changing into the adult form. Although a few amphibians spend their entire life in water, most live on land as adults.

All amphibians take in oxygen through their skin but just a few salamanders use *only* their skin to breathe. Other amphibians breathe with either lungs, gills, or gills and lungs in addition to their skin.

BIRDS

Birds are warm-blooded, just as mammals are. But feathers, not hair, help keep these animals warm. Feathers also allow birds to fly. Hollow or partially hollow bones make birds lighter in the air than they would be if they had heavier, denser, mammal-like bones. And struts inside the bones give the bones strength. Birds also have an efficient breathing system. They have two lungs with special balloonlike air sacs attached to each one. (For more about birds see *NatureScope—Birds, Birds, Birds!* [Vol. 1, No. 4].)

FISH

There are three major groups of fish: bony fish (e.g., bass, trout, and lungfish); cartilaginous fish (e.g., sharks, skates, and rays); and jawless fish (e.g., lampreys and hagfish). All fish are cold-blooded and most have scales covering their bodies. (Most bony fish have thin, overlapping scales; cartilaginous fish have non-overlapping scales that look like teeth; and jawless fish have slimy, unscaled bodies.) All fish breathe through gills and lay their eggs in water. And the young that hatch go through a larval stage before changing into adults. Most fish also have fins to help them swim and eyes located on the sides of their heads.

REPTILES

All of these cold-blooded vertebrates have scales that cover their bodies. But the scales are not always arranged in the same way. Some reptiles have a sheet of overlapping scales (lizards) and others have scales called *plates* that are found only in certain areas (tortoises). Many reptiles shed their skin several times during the year.

After laying their eggs, many reptiles abandon them. But some guard their eggs until they hatch. And with a few snakes and lizards the eggs hatch internally and the females give birth to live young.

VERTEBRATE CHARACTERISTICS GAME

After you've discussed the differences among the five vertebrate groups, have your kids use their knowledge in a running game. Here's how:

Divide the kids into two equal teams and have the teams line up, facing each other, on opposite sides of a field. (The teams should be about 50 feet [15 m] apart.) Next have the kids on each team count off and tell them to remember their numbers. (If you have an odd number of children, make the teams even by having one person be two different numbers.) Show the kids the five cut-outs that you made earlier and explain that each one represents one of the five vertebrate groups. Then line up the cut-outs in the center of the field between the two teams.

Explain that you will read a statement (see "Vertebrate Clues," below) that describes one or more vertebrate group. The kids must listen carefully and try to figure out which vertebrate group or groups you are describing. Explain that when you call out a number, the child on each team with that number must run to the center of the field and find the cut-out of that vertebrate group. Then each person must run back to his or her team before being tagged. For example, if you said, "These vertebrates have hollow bones . . . number five," the child with the number five on each team would run to the middle, try to grab the *bird* cut-out, and then run back "home." When one child grabs the bird cut-out, the other one may chase and try to tag him or her in order to score a point. (Some questions have more than one answer so each team can score two points if each grabs a correct cut-out.) Here's how to score:

- Grabbing the correct cut-out and making it home scores *two points.*
- Grabbing the *incorrect* cut-out and making it home scores *minus two points.*
- Grabbing the correct cut-out and getting tagged before reaching home scores *one point* for each team.
- Grabbing the *incorrect* cut-out and getting tagged before reaching home scores *minus one point* for each team.

At the end of each round have the kids return their cut-outs to the center of the field.

VERTEBRATE CLUES

1. These vertebrates have hollow bones. (birds)
2. These vertebrates are warm-blooded. (birds, mammals)
3. A turtle is an example of this group of vertebrates. (reptiles)
4. The largest animal ever to live is a member of this group. (mammals [blue whale])
5. These vertebrates are cold-blooded. (fish, reptiles, amphibians)
6. All of the vertebrates in this group breathe with gills. (fish)
7. Only these vertebrates have hair. (mammals)
8. These vertebrates never have claws and usually have four legs. (amphibians)
9. All of the vertebrates in this group nurse their young. (mammals)
10. This is the only group of vertebrates that has feathers. (birds)
11. These vertebrates have scales and lay eggs that usually have a leathery skin. (reptiles)
12. A few vertebrates in this group lay eggs, but almost all give birth to live young. (mammals)
13. Sweating helps keep many of the vertebrates in this group cool. (mammals)
14. These vertebrates have air sacs attached to their lungs. (birds)
15. Only these vertebrates have a muscular diaphragm that helps them fill their lungs with air. (mammals)
16. These vertebrates have the most fully developed brains. (mammals)
17. The vertebrates in this group have different kinds of teeth for eating different kinds of food. (mammals)
18. Many of these vertebrates have oil, milk, sweat, and scent glands in their skin. (mammals)
19. These vertebrates do not have teeth. (birds)

Mammals, Past and Present

Match clues to pictures of prehistoric mammals, then make a chart to compare prehistoric mammals with their modern relatives.

Objectives:
Describe several prehistoric mammals. Compare prehistoric mammals with their modern relatives.

Ages:
Intermediate and Advanced

Materials:
- *copies of pages 22, 23, 24, and 68*
- *easel paper*
- *markers*
- *scissors*
- *glue*
- *reference books*
- *different colored yarn*
- *tape*
- *paper punch*

Subject:
Science

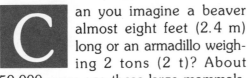

Can you imagine a beaver almost eight feet (2.4 m) long or an armadillo weighing 2 tons (2 t)? About 50,000 years ago these large mammals, as well as huge mammoths, saber-tooth cats, and others, roamed many parts of North America. In this activity your group will learn about these and other prehistoric mammals and then compare them with their modern mammal relatives.

Start by explaining that mammals have been around since the Age of Dinosaurs. Tell the kids that most paleontologists think the first mammals were small shrewlike creatures that were active mostly at night. For millions of years, mammals were dominated by dinosaurs and other reptiles. But when the dinosaurs became extinct, mammals began to branch out into many different species. Eventually they took over the dinosaurs' role as the dominant animals on earth. Some types of mammals that developed were evolutionary "dead ends," which means they died out leaving no living relatives. But others gave rise to the modern mammal groups that exist today.

Pass out copies of pages 22, 23, and 24 to each child. Explain that all of the mammals pictured on pages 22 and 23 are extinct. Read through the names of the mammals with the kids. (Some of these ancient mammals do not have common names. But for those that do, we've included their names in the clues on page 24.) Then tell them that each information block on page 24 matches one of the mammals on page 22 or 23. Have the kids cut out the pictures and the blocks of information *on the solid lines only.* Then have them try to match each mammal to one of the blocks of information. (Remind the kids to read the information blocks carefully—they contain a lot of clues! You might also want to pass out reference books. See page 93 for suggestions.)

Afterward go over the answers with the kids (see answers at the end of this activity) and then let them make their own mammal charts. Here's how:

Pass out markers and several sheets of easel paper to each person. Have the kids tape the sheets together end to end so that they form one large sheet about 17 inches (43 cm) wide and 70 inches (170 cm) long. Then have them draw a line down the center of their giant sheets and label the left-hand column "Mammals Past" and the right-hand column "Mammals Present." Next, have them glue down their prehistoric mammal pictures and information blocks in the left-hand column of their charts. They should glue them down in the following "groups" and then draw a line across the page beneath each one (see illustration). *Note:* Each group is made up of related mammals that the kids will be matching to a modern relative. (Explain that some groups are made up of a single mammal.)

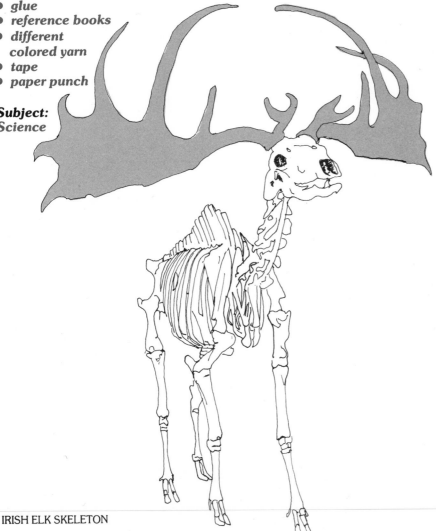

IRISH ELK SKELETON

- *Eremotherium, Glyptodon*
- *Castoroides*
- *Brontotherium, Hyracotherium (also called Eohippus), Moropus*
- *Aepycamelus, Dinohyus, Synthetoceras*
- *Uintatherium*
- *Mammuthus, Moeritherium, Amebelodon*
- *Hemicyon, Smilodon*
- *Hyaenodon*
- *Basilosaurus*
- *Diprotodon*

Afterward pass out copies of page 68 and have the kids cut out the pictures *on the solid lines only.* Explain that the nine modern mammals pictured represent eight different mammal groups called *orders* (horses and black rhinos are in the same order). Mammalogists have grouped mammals into about 20 different orders based on similar anatomy, physiology, ancestry, and other characteristics. Explain that most of the prehistoric mammal pictures they glued down are each distantly related to one of these modern mammal orders. Also explain that two of the prehistoric groups are evolutionary dead ends, so they don't have any modern relatives. (Uintatherium and Hyaenodon)

Have the kids try to guess the prehistoric/modern mammal matches. As they find a modern match, have them lay the pictures in the right-hand column across from the appropriate prehistoric group. (Remind them that two of the spaces in the right-hand column will be blank.)

After everyone is finished, use the information below to go over the kids' choices. Then have them glue down the modern mammal pictures in the correct places. (We've listed the matches and identified the modern orders in parentheses. We've also included the major characteristics of each order.)

- *Eremotherium, Glyptodon*—Armadillo (*Edentata:* Few or no teeth, large claws. Anteaters, armadillos, and sloths.)
- *Castoroides*—Prairie Dog (*Rodentia:* Chisel-like front teeth used for gnawing. Beavers, gophers, mice, porcupines, rats, squirrels, and others.)
- *Brontotherium, Hyracotherium, Moropus*—Black Rhinoceros, Wild Horse (*Perissodactyla:* Hooved feet with one or three toes. Asses, horses, rhinos, tapirs, and zebras.)
- *Aepycamelus, Dinohyus, Synthetoceras*—Camel (*Artiodactyla:* Hooved feet with two or four toes. Antelopes, bison, camels, deer, giraffes, goats, hippos, pigs, pronghorns, sheep, and others.)
- *Moeritherium, Amebelodon, Mammuthus*—Elephant (*Proboscidea:* Huge size, long trunk. Two species of elephants.)
- *Smilodon, Hemicyon*—Leopard (*Carnivora:* Special teeth for cutting meat. Bears, cats, civets, dogs, hyenas, raccoons, and weasels.)
- *Basilosaurus*—Dolphin (*Cetacea:* Live in water, front flippers, nostrils on top of head. Dolphins, porpoises, and whales.)
- *Diprotodon*—Kangaroo (*Marsupialia:* Young often carried in pouch. Kangaroos, koalas, opossums, wombats, and others.)
- *Uintatherium*—Dead end (no modern relatives)
- *Hyaenodon*—Dead end (no modern relatives)

(continued next page)

MAMMAL CHART

MAMMALS PAST	MAMMALS PRESENT
EREMOTHERIUM (eh-REE-moh-THIH-ree-um) — GLYPTODON (GLIP-tuh-don)	Armadillo
CASTOROIDES (cass-tuh-ROY-deez)	Prairie Dog
BRONTOTHERIUM (brahn-toh-THIH-ree-um) — HYRACOTHERIUM (high-RACK-oh-THIH-ree-um) — MOROPUS (MAWR-oh-pus)	Black Rhinoceros — Wild Horse

Answers:
1—Basilosaurus; 2—Moropus; 3—Glyptodon; 4—Synthetoceras; 5—Uintatherium; 6—Mammuthus; 7—Dinohyus; 8—Hyaenodon; 9—Diprotodon; 10—Brontotherium; 11—Smilodon; 12—Hyracotherium; 13—Moeritherium; 14—Eremotherium; 15—Amebelodon; 16—Hemicyon; 17—Castoroides; 18—Aepycamelus

BRANCHING OUT: MAMMALS THROUGH TIME

Now that the kids have learned about some prehistoric mammals, set up a time line so that they can see when these animals lived. Hang a long piece of yarn or string across the room and then tie seven short pieces of yarn to it at 10 million year intervals (see diagram). Then copy the chart (below) onto a chalkboard or large piece of easel paper and make a copy of pages 22 and 23. Cut up the pictures and put them into a bag.

Divide the kids into small groups and let each group choose two or three prehistoric mammals to place on the time line. Have them punch two holes in each picture and then thread a piece of yarn through the holes. (Tell the kids to use a different-colored piece of yarn for each picture.) The pieces of yarn should be long enough so that when the kids attach the two ends to the time line they span the amount of time that the mammal lived.

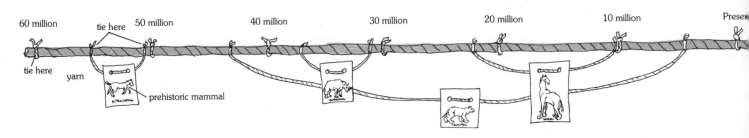

WHEN DID THEY LIVE ?

Hyracotherium	55-51 million years ago
Uintatherium	55-37 million years ago
Basilosaurus	43-37 million years ago
Moeritherium	43-32 million years ago
Hyaenodon	43-5 million years ago
Brontotherium	37-32 million years ago
Dinohyus	23-14 million years ago
Moropus	23-10 million years ago
Hemicyon	23-5 million years ago
Synthetoceras	23-3 million years ago
Aepycamelus	16-9 million years ago
Amebelodon	3-2 million years ago
Glyptodon	3 million-23,000 years ago
Smilodon	3 million-13,000 years ago
Mammuthus	2 million-11,000 years ago
Castoroides, Diprotodon, Eremotherium	2 million-10,000 years ago

Note: These time spans are approximations.

18

Fastest Land Mammals

Pronghorn
(runs about 55 miles per hour [mph] for short distances and about 35 mph for longer distances)

Cheetah
(runs about 60 mph for short distances)

Fastest Marine Mammal

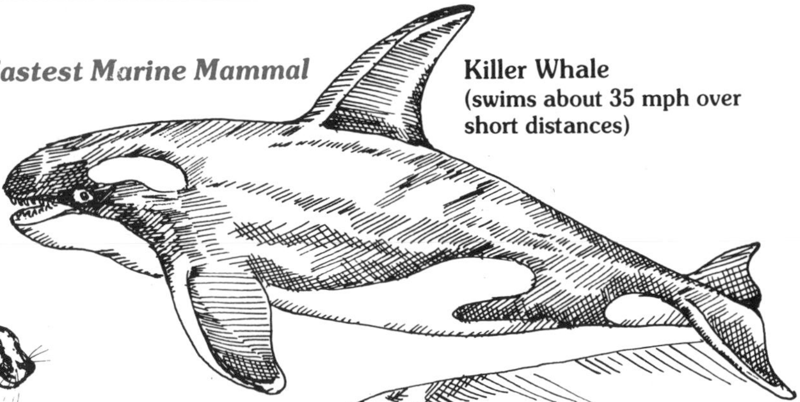

Killer Whale
(swims about 35 mph over short distances)

Best Breath Holders

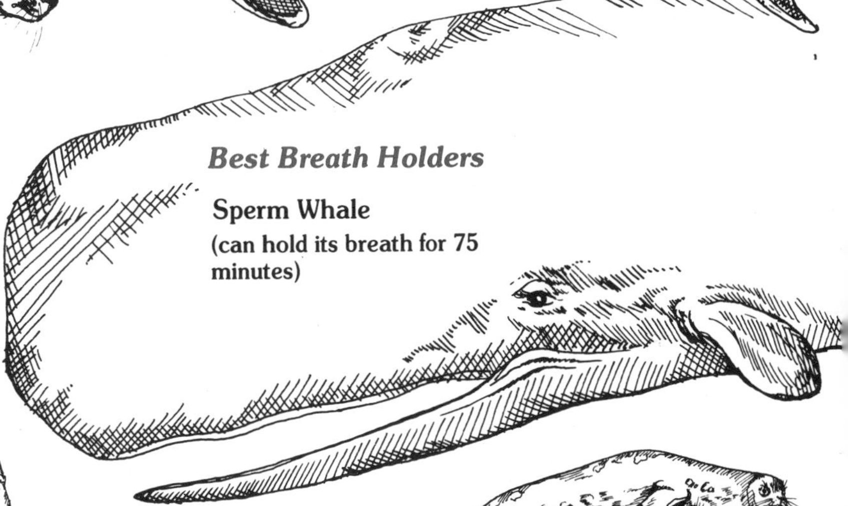

Sperm Whale
(can hold its breath for 75 minutes)

Best Jumpers

Jerboa
(can broad jump over 10 feet)

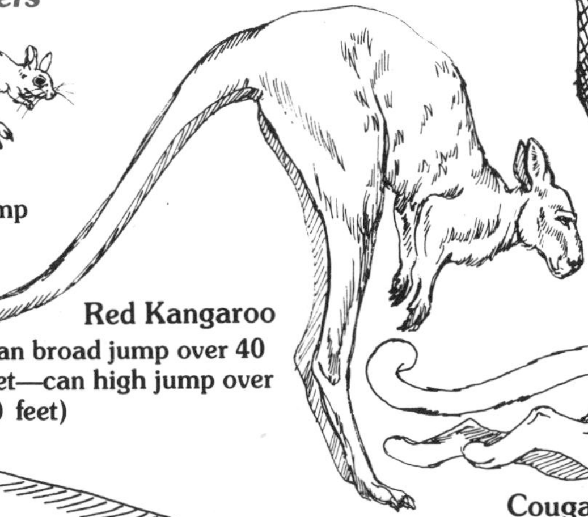

Red Kangaroo
(can broad jump over 40 feet—can high jump over 10 feet)

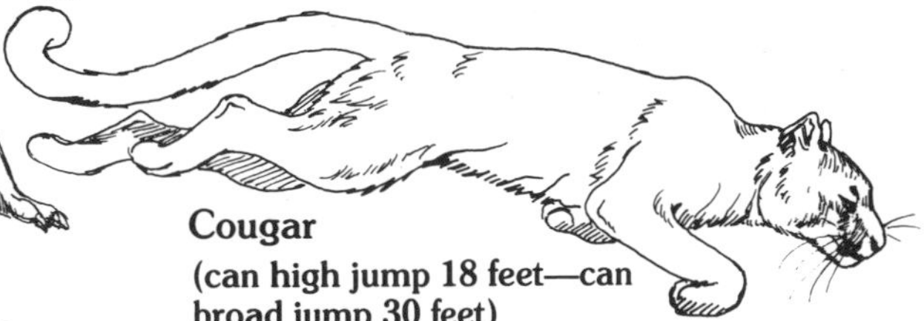

Cougar
(can high jump 18 feet—can broad jump 30 feet)

Weddell Seal
(can hold its breath for 60 minutes)

Largest Mammals

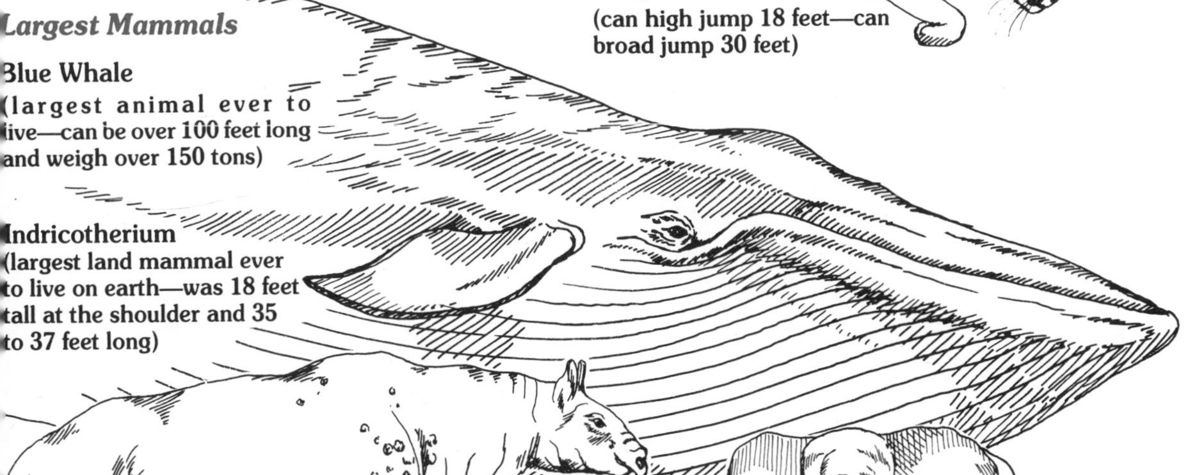

Blue Whale
(largest animal ever to live—can be over 100 feet long and weigh over 150 tons)

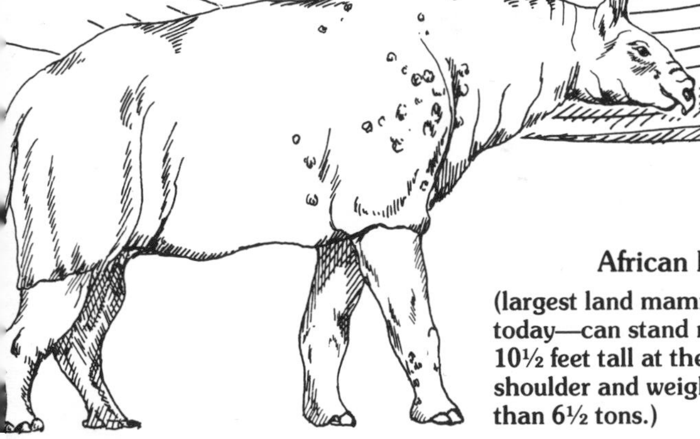

Indricotherium
(largest land mammal ever to live on earth—was 18 feet tall at the shoulder and 35 to 37 feet long)

African Elephant
(largest land mammal alive today—can stand more than 10½ feet tall at the shoulder and weigh more than 6½ tons.)

Giraffe
(tallest land mammal—can stand 19 feet high)

19

COPYCAT PAGE

THE LAYERED WOLF

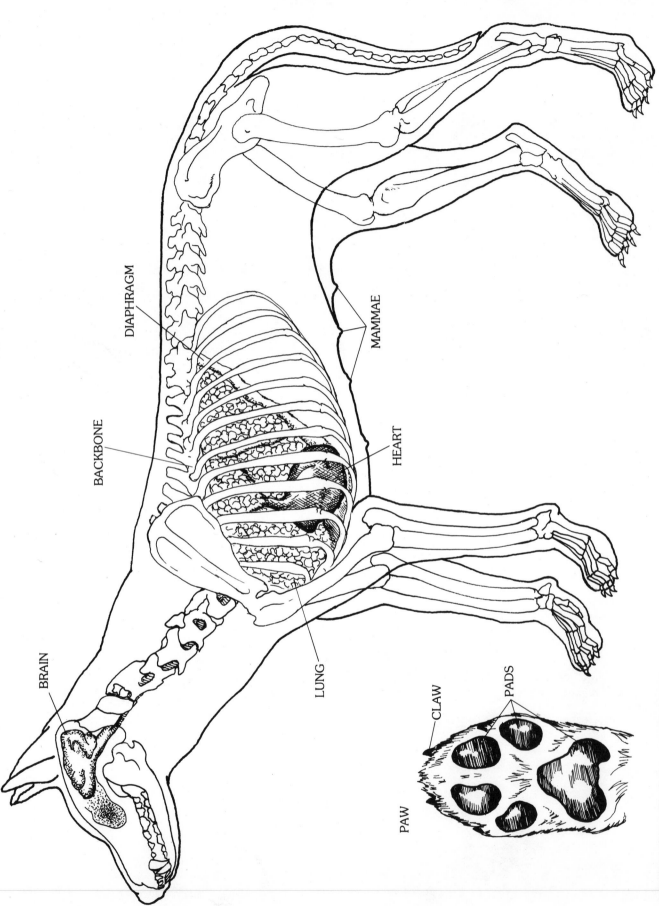

BRAIN

DIAPHRAGM

BACKBONE

MAMMAE

HEART

LUNG

CLAW

PADS

PAW

RANGER RICK'S NATURESCOPE: AMAZING MAMMALS

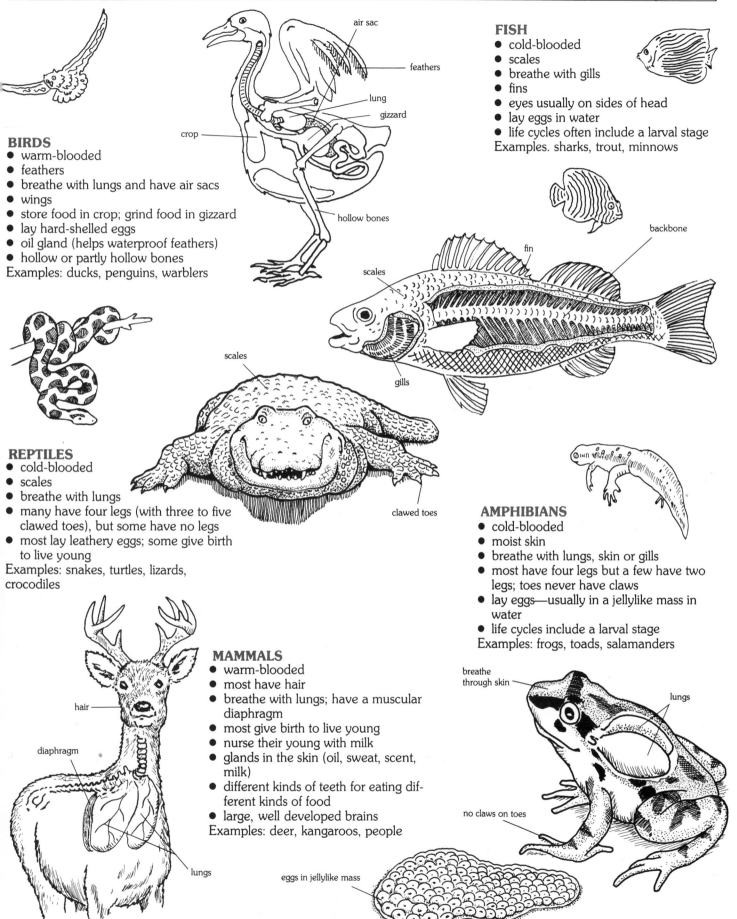

FISH
- cold-blooded
- scales
- breathe with gills
- fins
- eyes usually on sides of head
- lay eggs in water
- life cycles often include a larval stage

Examples. sharks, trout, minnows

feathers

air sac

lung

gizzard

crop

hollow bones

BIRDS
- warm-blooded
- feathers
- breathe with lungs and have air sacs
- wings
- store food in crop; grind food in gizzard
- lay hard-shelled eggs
- oil gland (helps waterproof feathers)
- hollow or partly hollow bones

Examples: ducks, penguins, warblers

backbone

fin

scales

scales

gills

REPTILES
- cold-blooded
- scales
- breathe with lungs
- many have four legs (with three to five clawed toes), but some have no legs
- most lay leathery eggs; some give birth to live young

Examples: snakes, turtles, lizards, crocodiles

scales

clawed toes

AMPHIBIANS
- cold-blooded
- moist skin
- breathe with lungs, skin or gills
- most have four legs but a few have two legs; toes never have claws
- lay eggs—usually in a jellylike mass in water
- life cycles include a larval stage

Examples: frogs, toads, salamanders

hair

diaphragm

lungs

MAMMALS
- warm-blooded
- most have hair
- breathe with lungs; have a muscular diaphragm
- most give birth to live young
- nurse their young with milk
- glands in the skin (oil, sweat, scent, milk)
- different kinds of teeth for eating different kinds of food
- large, well developed brains

Examples: deer, kangaroos, people

breathe through skin

lungs

no claws on toes

eggs in jellylike mass

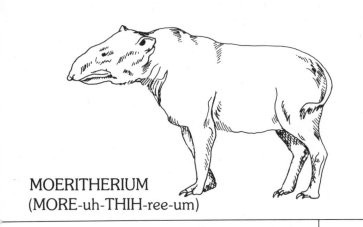

MOERITHERIUM
(MORE-uh-THIH-ree-um)

DIPROTODON
(die-PRO-tuh-don)

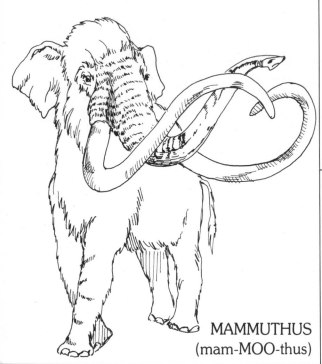

MAMMUTHUS
(mam-MOO-thus)

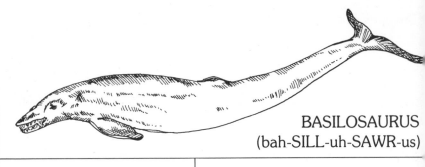

BASILOSAURUS
(bah-SILL-uh-SAWR-us)

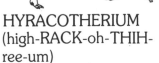

HYRACOTHERIUM
(high-RACK-oh-THIH-
ree-um)

GLYPTODON (GLIP-tuh-don)

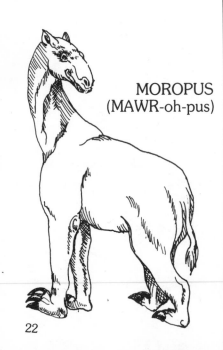

MOROPUS
(MAWR-oh-pus)

SYNTHETOCERAS
(sin-tha-TAH-sir-us)

DINOHYUS (die-noh-HIGH-us)

SMILODON (SMILE-uh-don)

RANGER RICK'S NATURESCOPE: AMAZING MAMM

UINTATHERIUM (YOU-in-ta-THIH-ree-um)

HEMICYON (hem-ee-SIGH-on)

AMEBELODON (am-a-BEEL-uh-don)

CASTOROIDES (cass-tuh-ROY-deez)

EREMOTHERIUM
(eh-REE-moh-THIH-ree-um)

HYAENODON (high-EE-nuh-don)

BRONTOTHERIUM
(brahn-toh-THIH-ree-um)

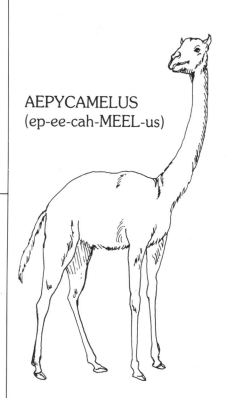

AEPYCAMELUS
(ep-ee-cah-MEEL-us)

e: These mammals are not drawn in proportion to each other.

Mammals, Past and Present

1
- ate fish
- had powerful, cutting cheek teeth
- was serpentlike and could grow to be 55 feet (16.5 m) long
- its nostrils were halfway up to the top of its head
- largest of the early whales
- lived in oceans near North America and Africa

2
- ate leaves, roots, and tubers
- might have used the claws on its front feet for defense, digging up roots and tubers, and grabbing and holding branches as it fed
- distantly related to horses
- also called Giant Pig
- lived in North America and Asia

3
- ate plants
- its bony shell protected it from enemies
- could use its bony tail as a club
- some were 10 feet (3 m) long and weighed 2 tons (2 t)
- related to armadillos
- lived in South, Central, and North America

4
- ate plants
- had short, curved horns between its ears
- had a Y-shaped nose horn
- related to deer and antelope
- also called Horned Camel
- lived in North America

5
- ate plants
- was about the size of a large rhinoceros and looked somewhat like one, but was not related
- had daggerlike canine teeth that grew down from its upper jaw
- had six horns on its head
- lived in North America

6
- ate plants
- some stood 14 feet (4 m) tall
- had huge tusks that curved up and back
- may have used its tusks for fighting rival males
- related to elephants
- also called Imperial Mammoth
- lived in southern North America

7
- ate dead animals, nuts, and fruits
- looked somewhat like a wild boar but was about the size of a large cow
- had long legs and was probably a fast runner
- distantly related to wild boars of Europe and Asia
- also called Giant Pig
- lived in North America and Asia

8
- ate meat
- was about the size of a wolf
- lived in North America, Europe, Asia, and Africa

9
- ate plants
- was largest marsupial ever to live
- was about the size of a hippopotamus
- its name means "two front teeth"
- lived in Australia

10
- ate leaves of trees and bushes
- was about the size of an Asian elephant
- looked somewhat like a rhinoceros but was not directly related
- may have used the Y-shaped horn on its snout for fighting rival males
- also called Thunder Beast
- lived in North America, Europe, and Asia

11
- ate meat
- was heavily built and fairly slow moving
- was about the size of a lion but had larger, more powerful front legs
- had two long, pointed canine teeth that hung down from its upper jaw
- also called Saber-tooth Cat
- lived in North and South America

12
- ate leaves
- was about the size of a small dog
- was the primitive ancestor of horses
- also called Dawn Horse
- lived in Europe and North America

13
- ate plants
- some were over 10 feet (3 m) long
- had a long body and short legs
- related to elephants and sea cows
- probably was semi-aquatic and lived in swamps
- lived in Africa

14
- ate tree leaves and twigs
- used its long, hooklike claws to pull down branches and to defend itself
- heavy and slow moving
- largest were as big as elephants
- related to sloths
- also called Giant Ground Sloth
- lived in South, Central, and North America

15
- ate plants
- used its long, shovel-like lower tusks for digging up roots
- was related to and looked somewhat like an elephant
- also called Shovel-tusker
- lived in North America

16
- ate meat
- was a large, bearlike dog
- also called Bear-dog
- lived in North America, Europe, and Asia

17
- ate water plants
- was almost 8 feet (2.4 m) long and weighed as much as a black bear
- lived in lakes and ponds
- was in the same family as beavers
- also called Giant Beaver
- lived in North America

18
- ate plants
- was almost as tall as a giraffe
- related to camels
- also called Giraffe-camel
- lived in North America

FAMILY LIFE

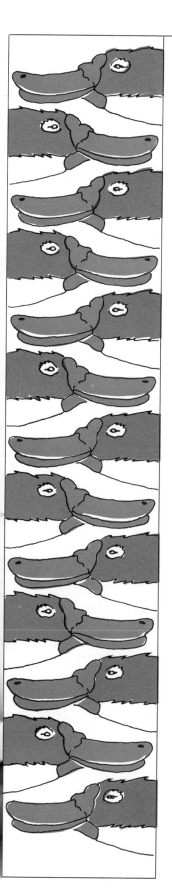

From the moment they're born, most insects, amphibians, reptiles, fish, and many other animals are completely on their own. Their parents don't stick around to raise them—and a lot of them don't survive to adulthood. But of the hundreds or thousands of eggs that many of the female parents produce, enough usually *do* survive to keep the species going.

Most birds and mammals do things differently. They usually don't have more than a few young at once, and they put a lot of energy into raising them. For months—or even years—they feed their offspring, protect them, and teach them how to survive. But it's among the mammals that family life reaches its greatest complexity.

In this chapter we'll focus on some of the different aspects of mammal family life—from the ways different species are born to the kinds of family groups young mammals grow up in. We'll also take a look at mammal "babysitters," "nurseries," and other family strategies and characteristics.

COMING INTO THE WORLD

Safe Inside: Among most kinds of animals, live birth is a real rarity and hatching from eggs is the rule. But with mammals, just the opposite is true. Most mammal embryos develop inside their mothers within an organ called the *womb,* or *uterus,* and after a certain period of time—called the *gestation period*—they're born. (See "Egg-ceptions to the Rule," on page 26, for a discussion of mammals that hatch from eggs.)

The majority of these "insiders" are known as *placental mammals.* Placental mammals are named for the *placenta,* an organ inside the uterus that's attached to the growing embryo. (Not all mammals that have a placenta are called placental mammals. See "Pocket Pals," below.) In placental mammals the placenta is attached to the embryo by several blood vessels that together make up the *umbilical cord.* The placenta absorbs oxygen and nourishment from the mother's blood, and from there the oxygen and nourishment flow through the umbilical cord to the embryo.

In general, the gestation periods of placental mammals are relatively long. With people, for example, it's nine months. But there's a wide range of variation—from 16 days in golden hamsters to 20 months or more in elephants!

Pocket Pals: Bandicoots, certain species of opossums, and a few other mammals share the record for the mammal with the shortest gestation period. Born after only 12 days or less, these animals belong to the group of mammals called *marsupials.* Kangaroos, koalas, wallabies, wombats, and many other mammals are also marsupials. Most female marsupials don't have as efficient a placenta as placental mammals do, and they don't have an umbilical cord either. (Nutrients and oxygen from the mother slowly pass through the marsupial placenta, and from there they pass directly into the fetus.) Also, most marsupial embryos don't spend as much time in their mothers' wombs as their placental counterparts do. Instead, most are born within a few weeks.

Newborn marsupials usually aren't much bigger than honey bees, and many are even smaller. They aren't nearly so well formed as placental mammals are at birth. But as tiny and undeveloped as it is, a newborn marsupial manages to crawl immediately into its mother's *marsupium*—the pocket, or pouch, on her belly. In the marsupium the infant grows quickly, attached firmly to a nipple. After a few weeks or months (depending on the species), it crawls out of the pouch—fully furred and with most of its senses developed—to take its first look at the world. (In some marsupials the pouch isn't very well developed—it's merely a fold of skin that encloses the mother's nipples. And in some marsupials there's no pouch at all. But whether there's a pouch or not, all marsupials crawl toward their mothers' abdomens and attach themselves to a nipple soon after birth.)

Egg-ceptions to the Rule: Instead of giving birth to live young as placentals and marsupials do, a few mammals—the *monotremes*—lay eggs. Only three monotreme species exist: the duck-billed platypus and two species of echidnas. (Echidnas, spine-covered animals that look something like hedgehogs, are sometimes called spiny anteaters. But they aren't related to hedgehogs or to ant-eaters.)

Monotreme eggs are flexible and leathery like reptile eggs—not hard and smooth like bird eggs. But unlike most reptiles (and like most birds), female monotremes incubate their eggs. Platypuses often curl up around their eggs to keep them warm. And echidnas carry their eggs around with them in a pouch on their bellies that develops only during the breeding season.

THE EARLY DAYS

Hairless and Helpless: Many placental mammals and all marsupials and monotremes are nearly hairless, almost helpless, and sometimes even blind when they're born. These infants, called *altricial* young, don't do much of anything for the first several days, weeks, or sometimes even months of their lives. Basically they just nurse, sleep, nurse some more—and grow. Like all mammals they grow

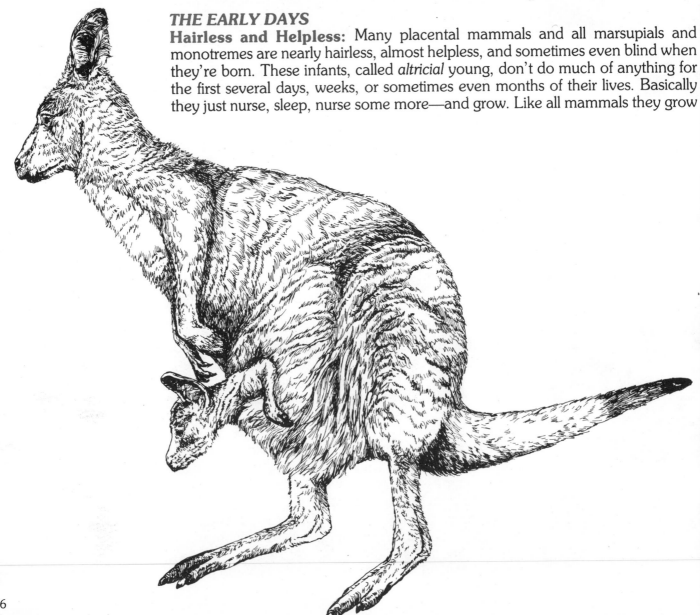

quickly, nourished by their mothers' high-energy milk. Human babies are altricial at birth, and so are newborn bats, platypuses, most mice, and many others.

A Place to Grow: To many young bears, foxes, and chipmunks, home is an underground burrow called a *den*. To young chimpanzees and gray squirrels it's often a leafy nest in the treetops. And to newborn rabbits it's often a fur-lined nest in a tangle of grasses. All of these mammal "nurseries" serve the same purpose: to protect the growing mammal from predators, bad weather, and other threats.

Some mammals share huge communal nurseries with others of their kind. For example, certain species of bats gather in caves by the thousands to give birth to their young. Despite incredible numbers of mother and infant bats—all crammed together on the nursery cave's ceiling and walls—a mother bat rarely loses her baby. (Some scientists think that the young of certain bat species have unique cries that their mothers key in on.)

Up and At 'Em: Not all mammals grow up in the safety of a den, nest, or other nursery. Antelope, deer, elephants, whales, and other mammals make their homes out in the open—in areas such as fields, plains, savannahs, or oceans. Most of these mammals are well developed at birth, with a full coat of hair (unless they're whales, elephants, or other "hairless" mammals) and with all five of their senses in good working order.

These *precocial* mammals can make a quick getaway soon after birth. Those that live on land can usually stand by the time they're a half hour old, and within just a few hours they can run. And most precocial marine mammals, such as dolphins and whales, can swim almost immediately.

GROWING UP

Learning to Live: Newborn mammals have a lot to learn before they become adults. In fact, learning usually plays a key role in a young mammal's life. That's not to say that mammals aren't born with *instinct*—the inherited information that tells an animal how to respond to certain situations. But in most cases their basic instincts are fine-tuned and enhanced by the things they learn throughout their lives—and especially when they're young.

Learning plays a role in the lives of other animals too—especially in the lives of birds—but in general not to the extent that it does with mammals. A long "childhood" gives a mammal more time to learn about its world and how to survive in it.

Bringing Up Baby: One of the ways young mammals learn is by watching and imitating adults. And a young mammal usually learns the most from its mother, since mammal mothers are often solely responsible for raising their offspring. Most mammal fathers, on the other hand, don't get involved with family duties—in fact, many never even come into contact with their young. A male may leave the female after mating, or the female may leave to search for a place to raise her future family.

But with some species the males do play a role in raising the young. Most male foxes, for example, bring food to their mates and pups. So do male dingoes, jackals, and some other mammals. (Dingoes and jackals are both types of wild dogs.)

A Family Affair: Some mammal parents, depending on the species, get a lot of help with the "kids" from others that they live with. For these mammals, the extended family is a way of life. Wolf packs, for example, are made up of anywhere from about 4 to about 20 animals, usually all of which are related. When parent wolves leave their pups to go on a hunt with the pack, one or two pack members often stay behind to "babysit." The same is true when a female lion with young goes hunting with others in her pride. And if a lion babysitter is a female with young of her own, she may even nurse the cubs that don't belong to her.

Super Babies!

Match pictures of baby mammals to descriptions of each one.

Objective:
Describe some interesting facts about several baby mammals.

Ages:
Primary

Materials:
- *copies of page 33*
- *crayons or markers*
- *scissors*
- *paper*
- *glue*
- *drawing paper (optional)*
- *reference books (optional)*

Subject:
Science

Ever heard of a baby that can walk within an hour after it's born? Baby wildebeests can. So can some baby deer, gazelles, and other grazers. Here's a way for your kids to learn about these and other amazing mammal baby feats.

Pass out copies of page 33 and explain that each of the descriptions in the "balloons" on the top half of the page goes with one of the mammal babies pictured on the bottom half. Tell the kids to color the mammal pictures and cut them out. Then have them cut out the balloons,

match them to the appropriate mammal pictures, and paste each baby mammal and its balloon onto another piece of paper.

You can extend the activity for older kids by having them find other amazing mammal baby facts once they've finished matching the mammals and balloons. The kids can draw pictures of the mammal babies, then write special facts about them at the tops of their pictures.

Answers:
1—giraffe; 2—zebra; 3—duck-billed platypus; 4—blue whale; 5—elephant; 6—red kangaroo

baby bobcats

Leonard Lee Rue III

Milk Is Amazing!

Make butter from cream.

Objectives:
Discuss some of the ways milk differs from one mammal species to another. Name several mammals from which people get milk. Describe how to make butter from cream.

Ages:
Primary and Intermediate

Materials:
- *chalkboard or easel paper*
- *whipping cream*
- *baby food jars with lids*

Here's an activity that will help your kids learn about milk, the special "baby food" that all mammals produce. Start by explaining that even though all mammals produce milk, the nutritional content of milk varies from one species to another. And each kind of mammal mother produces the kind of milk that's best suited to the needs of her young. For example, whales produce a super-rich, thick milk that's high in protein and fat. This special food helps young whales build up the insulating layer of blubber (fat) they are born with, keeping them warm in chilly waters. Ask the kids if they can explain why reindeer milk is also very rich in protein and fat. (Reindeer live on the tundra, a habitat that's often very cold. A reindeer mother's special milk

helps her young form the protective layer of fat they'll need to survive.)

To help your group see how the nutritional content of milk varies, copy the following chart on a chalkboard or large piece of easel paper:

KIND OF MAMMAL	% FAT IN MILK*	% PROTEIN IN MILK*
Camel	4.9	3.7
Cow	3.5	3.1
Goat	3.5	3.1
Human	4.5	1.1
Reindeer	22.5	10.3
Sheep	5.3	5.5
Water buffalo	10.4	5.5
Whale	35.0	13.0

*These figures are averages.

- *crackers or bread*
- *table knives for spreading homemade butter*

Subjects:
Science and Social Studies

Then explain that, besides containing fat and protein, the milk of different mammals also contains different amounts of vitamins, minerals, carbohydrates, and water. (Water is the main ingredient in all mammals' milk. For example, cow milk is about 87% water.)

Next ask the kids which of the mammals listed on the chart produces the milk that's sold in most stores. Then point out that, in some areas, people get milk from other mammals besides cows. In parts of Europe, for example, goats are the main milk producers. (Ask the kids if any of them have ever tasted goat milk. Can they describe what it tasted like?) In some parts of the Middle East sheep milk is popular, and in many desert areas camel milk is a mainstay. People drink water buffalo milk in Indonesia, and in Lapland

reindeer milk is a big part of some people's diets.

Next ask the kids if they can name some foods that are made from milk. (butter, cheese, cream, ice cream, yogurt, and so on) Explain that most of the milk products we're used to eating are made from cow milk. But a few milk products are made from the milk of other species. Ask if anyone has ever tasted goat milk cheese. (You might want to bring in some goat milk cheese and goat milk for the kids to sample. They're available at most health food stores.)

After talking about milk and milk products, have the kids make their own butter. Explain that the butter they get in stores is usually made from cream—the fatty liquid that's often removed from cow milk at milk processing plants. The kids will be making their butter from the heavy cream called whipping cream.

When the kids are ready to start "churning," give each person a baby food jar and lid. Fill each jar about one-third full of cream and tell the kids to shake their jars vigorously. Have them continue to shake as the cream thickens. (It'll take a lot of shaking, so you might want to have the kids work in pairs and take turns churning. If you're working with younger kids, you might want to demonstrate how to make butter rather than having all of the kids make their own. Each person could help churn the butter by giving the jar a few vigorous shakes.)

After about ten minutes (or less) of shaking, the kids' concoctions should start to look like whipped cream. And within another five minutes, the cream should become butter. You'll know the cream has reached the butter stage when the watery liquid called *whey* separates from the solid butter.

When the kids get to the butter stage, have them pour off the whey. Then let them sample their homemade butter on some crackers or bread.

Luise Woelflein

BRANCHING OUT: A TRIP TO THE DAIRY

After talking about milk and making butter, visit a local dairy to see how cows (or goats) are milked and how the milk is collected and stored.

Make a Baby Announcement

Fill in birth announcements for baby mammals.

Objective:
Name some characteristics of several baby mammals.

Ages:
Intermediate and Advanced

Materials:
- *copies of pages 34, 67, 68, and 69*
- *reference books*
- *crayons or markers*

Subject:
Science

Wouldn't it be exciting to receive birth announcements from mammals that live in different places around the world? In this activity your kids can create their own mammal birth announcements, then share them with the rest of the group. Start by passing out copies of page 34 and explaining that each person will be filling in his or her announcement with information about a particular mammal. Then make one copy each of pages 67, 68, and 69 and cut out the mammal picture squares. Put the squares into a bag and let each person pick one. (You might need to add the names of a few extra mammals on slips of paper if there aren't enough pictures to go around.)

Once everyone has a mammal to work with, tell the kids that they'll have some research time to fill in their announcements. Then go over the blanks on the announcement so the kids will get a feel for how they can fill them in. Explain that in the first blank they should fill in the name of the mammal they're working with. For example, if a person picked the picture of the wildebeest, he or she could write, "Mrs. Wildebeest" or "Wanda Wildebeest" in the first blank (see example #1). Point out that most mammal fathers don't play a role in raising the young. But some mammal fathers *do* play a role—and the kids should take this into consideration when they're filling in the first blank on their announcements. (Example #2 depicts the way an announcement for a red fox could be filled in. [Male red foxes help raise their young.])

Next tell the kids that their announcements should reflect the average number of young each person's mammal has at one time. (See the second blank in each example below.) Then tell the group that under the heading "Time of Birth," they can write either a specific month or a general season. Whatever they come up with should be based on the information they discover while they're doing their research.

You might want to lead a discussion about why mammals are born at certain times. For example, you could ask the kids why mammals that live in areas where there are four seasons usually give birth during the spring, and why mammals that live in arid areas usually give birth during the rainy season. (More food is available in spring or a rainy season, so young mammals and other animals born at these times have a better chance of surviving. And the mothers have more food to eat, which helps them produce a steady flow of milk.)

Now explain that, under "Place of Birth," each person should write the name of his or her mammal's habitat or special home. For example, if someone were filling in a birth announcement for a whitetail deer, he or she could simply write "the forest" under "Place of Birth." A beaver's place of birth, on the other hand, could read "a lodge in our beaver pond."

Finally, tell the kids that when they draw their pictures of the parents they should keep in mind that many adult male and female mammals look different from one another. For example, some males have tusks, manes, antlers, and so on.

When the kids have finished filling in their announcements and drawing pictures of the young and adults, have them fold the announcements over and draw more pictures on the outside. Then have them present their announcements to the rest of the group.

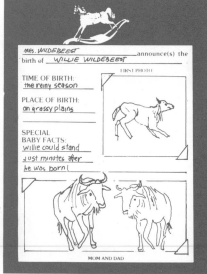

EXAMPLE #1

EXAMPLE #2

Family Password

Play a game about mammal family life.

Objectives:
Compare the family lives of several mammals. Describe several ways mammal babies differ.

Ages:
Intermediate and Advanced

Materials:
- *chalkboard or easel paper*
- *reference books*
- *index cards*
- *clues on page 32*

Subject:
Science

By playing "Family Password" your kids can learn more about how different kinds of mammal babies grow up. Begin the activity by talking about how monotreme, marsupial, and placental mammals are born and how they develop. (See the background information on pages 25-27.) After the discussion, list the following mammals on a chalkboard or large piece of easel paper: giraffe, gray wolf, cougar, bottle-nosed dolphin, black bear, African elephant, fruit bat, nine-banded armadillo, human, whitetail deer, Virginia opossum, red kangaroo, duck-billed platypus, leopard seal, killer whale.

Divide the group into two teams, and explain that the members of each team must find out the following information about each mammal listed:

- size, appearance, and number of young at birth
- whether the mammal is a monotreme, marsupial, or placental
- type of family group the young live in, if any
- who helps raise the young (mother and/or father, other members of group)
- where the young are born and raised (in a den or nest, on the open savannah, and so on)
- what the young eat after they are weaned
- any other neat facts about family life

Pass out index cards and tell the kids to record the information they find out about each mammal on a separate card. (Team members can gather information on each of the mammals listed, or divide the mammals up among the group.) Then supply the kids with reference books, and give them time to complete their research.

HOW TO PLAY THE GAME

Have the two teams sit on opposite sides of the room and tell them they will be playing a password-like game. To help the kids remember which mammals are included in the game, put the list of mammals from the first part of the activity where everyone can see it.

Explain to the kids that you have a set of five clues for 10 of the mammals listed. (There are five extra mammals that will not match any of the clues.) The first clue in each set is worth five points, the second clue is worth four points, and so on. The object of the game is to be the first team to figure out which mammal fits each clue (or clues) and thus score the most points.

Have the teams pick a number to see who goes first. Then read the first clue in the first set to team #1. Encourage the team members to discuss the clue before answering. If they answer correctly, they receive five points. If they give a wrong answer, read the second clue, worth four points, to team #2. If they miss, read the third clue, worth three points, to team #1. Continue reading clues for decreasing point values until the kids name the correct mammal.

Then start the next set of clues. (This time, give team #2 a chance to answer first.) Continue playing the game until you've gone through all the clues. The team with the most points at the end of the game wins.

DUCK-BILLED PLATYPUS

1. My mom seals herself inside her nesting chamber by plugging up the entrance with soil.
2. I can store worms, insects, and other food in my cheek pouches.
3. I get milk from my mom—even though she doesn't have nipples.
4. Watch out for the sharp spurs on my dad's hind feet—they're poisonous!
5. Before I come into the world, my mom incubates me for about 10 days.

BOTTLE-NOSED DOLPHIN

1. Without a push from my mom, I'd never get my first breath of air.
2. I can whistle for my mom only a few seconds after I'm born.
3. At birth, I look almost exactly like my mom—but I'm only one-third of her length!
4. I'm born fluke-first.
5. A tasty fish will probably be my first solid meal.

GIRAFFE

1. One or two babysitters usually stay with us kids while our moms browse.
2. Hungry members of the cat family are the main reason that I may not live to celebrate my first birthday.
3. Although I'll get a lot bigger as I grow older, the pattern of my coat will never change.
4. At birth, I'm only knee-high to my mom—but I'm taller than the average person.
5. My life begins with a five-foot (1.5-m) fall.

AFRICAN ELEPHANT

1. I have two front teeth that will grow throughout my life.
2. As I grow up, I'll have a lot of company. My mom, aunts, and cousins will take turns watching me.
3. If I'm a male, I'll eventually leave home. But if I'm a female, I'll never leave home.
4. I may live to be about 70 years old.
5. My mom was pregnant for nearly two years before I was born.

WHITETAIL DEER

1. When danger is near, I flash part of my body.
2. It's not unusual for me to have a twin brother or sister.
3. When I'm very young, predators can't smell me because I have no scent.
4. The pattern of my coat changes as I grow older.
5. If I'm a male I'll have velvet.

GRAY WOLF

1. I probably won't go outside until I'm about eight weeks old.
2. I'm deaf and blind when I'm born.
3. My parents have a lot of help raising me.
4. My first solid meal will probably be meat that has already been chewed by my parents.
5. Through play, my brothers and sisters and I learn the social rules of our pack.

NINE-BANDED ARMADILLO

1. I usually have three sisters *or* three brothers—but I never have sisters *and* brothers.
2. I'm pretty soft-skinned when I'm first born—but I toughen up as I get older.
3. I'm born at a time when lots of juicy worms and insects are around.
4. I can cross rivers and streams by swallowing air to help me float.
5. In the United States, my kind is no longer found just in the West. We've spread into parts of the Southeast too!

VIRGINIA OPOSSUM

1. My brothers and sisters and I compete for something right after we're born—and the losers die.
2. I won't see much of the world until I'm at least two months old.
3. My mom was pregnant with me for about 13 days.
4. I can really get on my mom's back!
5. My tail is hairless and looks something like a rat's tail.

RED KANGAROO

1. I won't move around on my own until I'm about six months old.
2. Right after I'm born, I have to make a long journey for my first meal.
3. My relatives are members of a mob.
4. When I'm born, I'm about the size of a lima bean.
5. You can call me "joey."

HUMAN

1. I can be born during any month of the year.
2. Both mom and dad take care of me.
3. Even after I'm full-grown, I won't have as much hair as most mammals have.
4. By the time I'm three years old, I'll eat all kinds of food—from meat to fruits to vegetables.
5. I probably won't leave home until I'm at least 18 years old.

1.
I fall five feet to the ground when I'm born!

2.
I can run and play only an hour after I'm born!

3.
I did something most mammals can't do: I hatched from an egg!

4.
I weigh three tons at birth. And I'll gain about 200 pounds a day just by drinking my mother's milk!

5.
Before I'm born, I grow inside my mother for almost two years. That's a record!

6.
I'm no bigger than a penny when I'm born. But when I grow up I'll be as tall as a fully-grown person!

Duck-billed Platypus	Giraffe	Elephant

Blue Whale	Red Kangaroo	Zebra

RANGER RICK'S NATURESCOPE: AMAZING MAMMALS

A BABY ANNOUNCEMENT

_____ announce(s) the

birth of _____.

TIME OF BIRTH:

_____

PLACE OF BIRTH:

_____

_____

SPECIAL BABY FACTS:

_____

_____

_____

FIRST PHOTO

_____

MOM AND DAD

STAYING ALIVE AND FITTING IN

How is a red kangaroo like an American bison? At first glance these two animals don't seem to have much in common, aside from the fact that they're both large mammals. After all, kangaroos are marsupials and bison are placentals. Kangaroos hop from place to place, whereas bison run along on all fours. And they live about as far away from each other as two animals can.

But as different as they are, these two animals fill a similar *ecological niche*—that is, they perform a similar "job," or function, in each of their habitats. The red kangaroo fills the role of a large grazer—munching grass on the dry plains of Australia. And the American bison does the same job—but on a different continent.

Just like bison and red kangaroos, all other mammals fill special niches in the habitats where they live. From plant eater to predator to scavenger, each is adapted to a certain way of life. In this chapter we'll look at some of the many ways mammals are adapted to living in their habitats, including how they get their meals, defend themselves, and stay alive from one season to the next.

FINDING FOOD

The Hunters and the Hunted: The way mammals—and all other animals—live has a lot to do with the kind of food they eat. Kangaroos and bison are examples of *herbivores,* or animals that feed on plants. Specifically, they're *grazers,* which means that they eat mostly grasses. Herbivores that *browse* specialize more on the leaves, stems, twigs, and bark of shrubs and trees. Deer are browsers, and so are giraffes, koalas, and some voles.

Herbivores and many other kinds of mammals often become meals for *carnivores*—animals that eat meat. Some carnivores, such as lions, weasels, and wolves, usually hunt and kill other animals for their meals. Others, such as jackals and hyenas, do some hunting but also eat a lot of *carrion* (the remains of animals that are already dead).

An Insect a Day...: Moles, shrews, pangolins, many bats, and some other mammals are *insectivores* (animals that eat insects and other small invertebrates almost exclusively). Some insectivores, such as anteaters, specialize in eating a particular kind of insect. But many shrews, moles, and other insectivores eat a variety of insects, as well as earthworms, centipedes, millipedes, and spiders.

A Varied Diet: Mammals that are *omnivores* eat a wide range of foods—from grasses and fruits to fresh meat and carrion. Omnivores have an advantage over strict herbivores, carnivores, and others that specialize in eating certain kinds of food: If one food source becomes scarce, they can easily shift to another source without feeling much of a "pinch." (Most omnivores change their diets periodically, according to the season and the availability of certain foods.) Bears, opossums, raccoons, and humans are all *omnivorous* mammals.

All Kinds of Eaters: At the other end of the spectrum from omnivorous mammals are mammals that eat only one type of food (or a couple of different types). Vampire bats, for example, lap blood for their meals. Fruit bats and some other mammals eat fruit. Other bats and some possums eat pollen and nectar. And certain whales and other marine mammals feed mostly on the tiny sea animals called *krill.*

(continued next page)

But no matter what they feed on, all mammals have special adaptations that help them make the most of what they eat. For example, a giraffe's long neck helps it browse on leaves high in the treetops. Because giraffes can feed in places that are out of reach for most mammals, they avoid competing with other browsers for food.

SURVIVING

The Best Defense: Like other animals, most mammals face a lot of dangers throughout their lives. One danger many mammals face every day is the possibility of becoming a hungry animal's meal. Most mammals try to avoid this fate by running away (or, depending on the species, by swimming or flying away). Small mammals—mice and squirrels, for example—usually try to run to a safe place, such as a burrow in the ground or a hole in a tree. Deer, antelope, and most other large mammals usually just keep running until their pursuers get tired and give up the chase. But if running away doesn't work and a mammal finds itself face to face with a predator, it may bite, scratch, kick, or do anything else it possibly can to protect itself.

Special "Tricks": Certain physical features and ways of behaving help some mammals defend themselves. A porcupine's quills can intimidate most predators, and so can a skunk's smelly spray. A hare's white winter coat can make it hard to see against a snowy background. And an opossum's habit of playing dead (actually a kind of involuntary paralysis) can trick most hungry animals into letting it alone. (Many predators quickly lose interest in an animal that suddenly stops moving—unless they've just killed the animal themselves.)

Group living can also be a good defense. A mammal that lives in a herd, colony, or other group has less chance of being attacked by a predator than if it lives alone. And the first group member to sense danger usually alerts other members by stamping the ground, giving an alarm call, or signaling in some other way. For example, when a prairie dog spies a coyote, golden eagle, or other predator, it barks an alarm call and dives into the nearest burrow. The other prairie dogs in the colony stop what they're doing and also scamper into burrows—even if they haven't seen the danger themselves.

Escaping the Elements: Most of us probably think of birds when we think of animals that migrate. But many mammals migrate too, and for the same reasons that birds do: to avoid seasonal food (and/or water) shortages, to escape harsh weather conditions, and in some cases to raise their young.

The distances mammals migrate vary from one species to the next. For example, gray whales in the northern Pacific Ocean begin a 5000 to 6000-mile (8000 to 9600-km) journey to warm waters off the coast of Mexico in early fall. And when drought dries up the African grasslands and waterholes, tens of thousands of wildebeests, zebras, and other mammals often migrate to "greener pastures" hundreds of miles away. But some mammals don't go very far at all. Bighorn

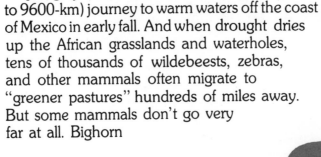

sheep in the Rocky Mountains, for example, travel down to valleys after spending the warm months grazing in high mountain pastures. Chamois in the European Alps and vicuñas in South America's Andes also migrate with the seasons from the highlands to the valleys.

Toughing It Out: Even though most habitats have food shortages, severe weather, or other harsh conditions at one time or another, most species of mammals don't migrate. Instead, they have other ways of toughing out the bad times. Some rodents and other mammals *cache* (store) food, then eat it later when finding food becomes difficult. Other mammals shift their diets when a change in the seasons makes some foods scarce.

Chipmunks, prairie dogs, some bats, and other mammals avoid tough winter conditions altogether by hibernating. During this deep winter "sleep," a mammal's whole system slows down. Its main source of food—a large amount of stored fat—usually tides it over until spring, when food becomes available again and the mammal comes out of hibernation. (There's a lot of variation in how deeply different "winter sleepers" actually sleep. Some, such as some ground squirrels, wake up from time to time. But others, such as some marmots, usually stay unconscious from the moment they go into hibernation until spring arrives—a period that may span six months or longer.)

A few mammals that live in deserts or other hot, dry places also fall into a deep sleep—but this condition, called *estivation,* is triggered by food shortages brought on by drought. Hibernation, on the other hand, occurs when cold-weather food shortages set in. (For more about estivation, see "When the Time Is Right" on page 26 of *NatureScope—Discovering Deserts* [Vol. 1, No. 5].)

THE BIG PICTURE

How do mammals "fit into" their habitats? Like birds, insects, reptiles, amphibians, and other animals, they're an integral part of *ecological communities.* Most communities are made up of all kinds of different animals—not just mammals, or birds, or insects, or any other single group. And the different kinds of mammals and other animals that live in a community are constantly interacting with one another—and with the community's plants. In a meadow community, for example, small mammals called meadow voles make nests in meadow grasses and eat and spread seeds of meadow plants. Foxes, weasels, and non-mammal predators such as snakes, hawks, and owls eat the voles, mice, and other small animals. Together, all of the plants and animals in a community—mammals included—form a working, interdependent system.

Mammals on the Move

Imitate the movements of different mammals by playing follow the leader, mammal-style.

Objective:
Give some examples of how different mammals move.

Ages:
Primary and Intermediate

Materials:
- *pictures of different mammals (see activity for suggestions)*
- *slips of paper*

Subjects:
Science and Physical Education

Here's an active way to teach your kids about how different mammals get around. Begin by asking why mammals need to move. (to find food, escape from predators, find a mate) Then use the background information below and pictures of appropriate mammals to discuss the different ways mammals move. After you talk about each category, have the kids practice the movements we suggest. Then play follow the leader, mammal-style. Here's how:

Choose one of the children to be the leader and have the rest of the group line up behind him or her. (With younger children, you might want to have an adult leader throughout.) Tell the kids to leave an arm's length of distance behind the person in front of them.

Now ask the leader to choose one of the mammals you've discussed and then move forward imitating that mammal. The rest of the group should follow in a line, making the same movement.

After a few minutes, tell the "train" to stop, and have the leader run to the back of the line. Let the new leader (the next person in line) choose another mammal from the discussion and act it out. Then have everyone imitate the leader. Continue until everyone has had a chance to be the leader—or until the kids are too tired to move!

HOW MAMMALS GET AROUND

Luise Woelflein

Walkers and Runners: Most mammals walk and run on all four legs—but different mammals use different parts of their feet when they move. Show the kids a picture of a bear and explain that it walks and runs on "flat" feet (the soles of its feet) just as people, raccoons, skunks, and porcupines do. Other mammals, such as wolves, dogs, and cats, walk and run on their toes (the pads of their feet). And deer and other hooved mammals actually walk on their toenails! (Have the kids move around on their hands and feet. They can alternate between placing their palms and soles flat on the ground [bear] and letting only their fingertips and toes touch [wolf].)

Jumpers: Mammals such as kangaroos cover a lot of ground by making long leaps. Show the group a picture of a kangaroo, pointing out its large hind legs, long tail, and small forelimbs. Explain that a kangaroo uses its strong hind legs for jumping, its tail for balance, and its weaker forelimbs for holding food. (Have the kids hold their arms close to their chests and jump forward.)

Diggers: Some mammals spend all or most of their lives underground. Point out the broad forelimbs and strong claws of a mole. Like badgers, hedgehogs, and most other digging mammals, moles use their front limbs for digging through soil. (Have the kids walk on their knees and move their arms in a breast stroke motion to simulate pushing dirt away.)

Swingers: Mammals that live in trees also depend on strong forelimbs. For ex-

Luise Woelflein

ample, gibbons have muscular grasping hands and long strong arms that help them swing from branch to branch. (Have the kids raise their hands above their heads, reaching one arm forward at a time to grab "branches" as they walk.)

Gliders: Some other tree-dwelling mammals get around by gliding. Flying squirrels, sugar gliders, and a few other mammals have flaps of skin connecting their front and hind legs. As they leap into the air, these skin flaps spread out to form a furry parachute. (Have the kids "glide" by holding their arms straight out to their sides, keeping them steady as they walk.)

Fliers: Bats are the only mammals that can fly. Show the kids a close-up picture of a bat wing, pointing out the long finger bones that are connected with thin skin. Explain that a bat uses its small hind legs for hanging upside-down when it is resting. (Have the kids flap their arms.)

Swimmers: Aquatic mammals such as porpoises and whales are specialized for swimming. Their forelimbs have evolved into powerful flippers, which help them steer as they swim. Their hind legs gradually disappeared as they evolved and their flattened tails give them the push that propels them through the water. (Have the kids keep their legs close together, hold their upper arms straight down to the side, and move their forearms up and down as they take tiny steps.)

BRANCHING OUT: FIND YOUR PARTNER

Try moving as these mammals do:
- kangaroo
- mole or badger
- gorilla
- rabbit or hare
- deer
- bat
- flying squirrel
- sloth
- elephant
- bear
- skunk
- mouse
- cheetah
- monkey
- porpoise

For this mammal movement game, you'll need an even number of players and an open area outside or inside. Before starting the game, choose 15 mammals (see sample list) that move in distinctive ways and copy each name onto two separate slips of paper. (You will end up with two identical groups of mammals.) Then put each set of slips into a separate bag. (Adjust the number of slips to equal the number of players in your group.)

Now divide the group into two equal teams. Give each team one bag, and have each person pick a slip of paper from the bag. Tell the kids not to say what mammals they've picked.

Next take the group to the playing area

and have the teams form two lines facing each other. (The teams should be about 60 feet [18 m] apart.) Explain that each person has a partner on the opposite team and the object of the game is for each person to match up with his or her partner. When you say "go," everyone should start moving like the mammal on his or her slip and head toward the other team. When the two partners find each other, they should sit down together and wait until everyone else has paired up. (You can also have the kids mimic the sounds that their mammals make to help both teams find their partners.) Play a few rounds so the kids can imitate some different mammals.

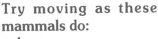

Mammal Safari

Take a walk to look for signs of mammals.

Objective:
Describe several signs that show that mammals have been in the area.

Ages:
Primary, Intermediate, and Advanced

Materials:
- *pieces of cardboard*
- *pencils*
- *paper*
- *rubber bands*
- *field guides*

Subject:
Science

Tracks, burrows, droppings, dens, nests, and many other signs show that mammals are or have been in an area. In this activity your group can look for these and other mammal signs.

First have the kids make simple clipboards by attaching paper to pieces of cardboard with rubber bands. Then explain that they will be going on a mammal safari to search for signs of mammals.

Adapt the safari according to the age of your group. You can take younger kids out on a group hike, stopping along the way to point out any mammal signs you find. They can try to sketch the signs they see, or they can try to draw some of the mammals that might live in the area. Older kids can scout an area in pairs, sketching what they find and jotting down notes. You might want to set a time limit and have everyone meet inside afterward. Have the kids use field guides to identify signs they didn't know. Then take some time to talk about what everyone has seen, making a list of the mammals that live in your area.

You might want to go over the following tips before you start your mammal trek to give your group a better idea of what to look for.

Homes: Mammal homes can be almost anywhere—in trees; under the ground; along streams, rivers, and ponds; in grassy fields; along cliffs; in caves; and so on. Here are a few home-finding tips:

- Entrances to burrows and dens may have soil scraped away or piled up in unusual ways.
- Many homes, such as fox or skunk dens, have characteristic odors.
- Look in trees for leafy squirrel nests and for hollowed-out trunks where a den might be located. Droppings at the base of a tree may be a clue that a tree-dwelling mammal such as a porcupine or raccoon found shelter there.
- A few mammals, such as beavers and muskrats, build homes that are easy to spot once you know what to look for.
- Keep an eye out for raised ridges of soil or mounds of earth where moles and pocket gophers may have tunneled.

Resting Spots: Some mammals leave shallow depressions where they've lain down to rest. Rabbits leave small *forms* in brushpiles or brushy areas. Deer leave larger depressions in grass, soil, or snow.

Food Clues: Squirrels often leave broken nutshells or shredded pine cones where they've been eating. Other clues to munching mammals are bark stripped from trees (deer), small branches trimmed from trees (porcupines), broken branches in berry patches (bears), and stem tips nipped off by browsers (deer, rabbits). (Rabbits usually browse on low-growing stems, leaving a neatly cut diagonal tip. Deer tend to browse on higher stems, leaving uneven tips.)

Droppings: Although kids may be a bit squeamish about looking at mammal droppings, these materials can sometimes be great clues for identifying what mammals were out and about. Check in field guides for descriptions, drawings, and pictures of mammal "scat."

young albino raccoon

Rubs, Scrapes, and Scratches: Large mammals, such as bears and deer, sometimes leave hair and broken branches behind in places where they stop to mark their scent. Male deer (bucks) often thrash their antlers in brush, getting ready for the mating season. In the proc- ess, they strip the velvet from their antlers. And wild and domestic cats often leave scratch marks on trees.

Tracks: See "Tricky Tracks" on page 45 for tips on identifying mammals by their tracks.

A Menu for Mammals

Match different mammals to the foods they would most likely eat.

Objectives:
Give some examples of mammals and the foods they eat. Define herbivore, carnivore, and omnivore.

Ages:
Intermediate

Materials:
- *copies of page 48*
- *reference books*
- *pencils or pens*
- *chalkboard or easel paper*

Subject:
Science

Some mammals will eat just about anything! Opossums will devour insects, worms, fruits, corn, birds, snakes, frogs, and the remains of road-killed animals. And spotted hyenas will gobble up everything from the animals that they kill themselves to the leftovers of other predators' kills to garbage from nearby villages.

But unlike these general feeders, other mammals will eat only specific types of food. For example, koalas thrive on an exclusive diet of eucalyptus leaves. And vampire bats live only on the blood that they lap up from other mammals and some birds. By matching some of the more specialized feeders to their "favorite" foods, your kids can learn about the variety of foods that mammals eat and how certain mammals are adapted to eating certain types of food.

Begin the activity by asking the kids to name their favorite kinds of food. List their choices on a chalkboard or a large piece of easel paper. Then take a look at the completed list. There will probably be a wide variety of foods, ranging from ice cream to steak.

Next explain to the kids that people and some other mammals, such as bears, opossums, and raccoons, eat a wide variety of foods and are called *omnivores*. Using the information under "Finding Food" on page 35, talk about omnivores and the other kinds of eaters that exist among mammals—from *herbivores* to *carnivores* to super-specialists that eat only one or a couple of different foods. Also use the information under "Snip, Grind, and Stab" on page 4 to discuss the fact that mammal teeth help different mammals eat different foods.

After the discussion, pass out a copy of page 48 to each child. Explain that each of the mammals illustrated on the page has a pretty specialized diet. Then have the kids look at the menu in the center of the page. Explain that each menu item matches the food preference of one of the mammals pictured.

Tell the kids they may use reference books if they don't know what each mammal eats. Then have them write the number of each menu item next to the appropriate mammal's name. (Explain to the kids that the menu items are funny ways of describing what these mammals eat. For example, a lynx preys on squirrels—but it doesn't really eat squirrel fritters! And although we've listed the items under breakfast, lunch, and dinner, this doesn't mean mammals eat those foods at specific times.)

When everyone's finished, go over the page and discuss the different type of food each mammal eats using the answers below.

Answers:
1—koala; 2—long-nosed fruit bat; 3—fisher; 4—lynx; 5—humpback whale; 6—aardvark; 7—cheetah; 8—sea otter; 9—elephant

Habitats for Sale

Write classified ads for mammal homes and habitats. Draw mammal habitat pictures.

Objectives:
Define habitat. Describe how different kinds of mammals are adapted to living in certain habitats.

Ages:
Intermediate

Materials:
- *copies of pages 67, 68, and 69*
- *reference books*
- *scissors*
- *paper and pencils*
- *construction paper*
- *glue*
- *crayons or markers*

Subject:
Science

Mammals live in almost every type of habitat on earth—from rain forests to oceans to deserts. In this activity, your kids will discover what a habitat is and how mammals, like all animals, are adapted to living in certain types of habitats.

Start by introducing the word *habitat* to your group. Explain that an animal's habitat is the place where it lives and which provides the food, water, shelter, and space it needs to survive. Ask the kids to name different habitats where mammals live. For example, they might say fields, forests, oceans, deserts, streams, coasts, rain forests, and so on. Then ask the kids to name some of the mammals that live in each of these habitats.

Next explain that some mammals build special homes in their habitats. The homes provide shelter from weather, protection from enemies, and a place to raise their young. Have the children name some specific mammal homes. (beaver lodges, squirrel nests, fox dens, chipmunk burrows, prairie dog burrows, and so on) Point out that many mammals, such as lions, antelope, deer, and others, do not build special homes.

Now ask if anyone knows what a classified ad is. (You might want to read a few ads from a newspaper's classified section.) Then read them this make-believe example and ask them to guess what mammal might want to buy this type of habitat:

Great Grasslands: Prime grassland available in Africa. Loaded with antelope, springboks, zebras, and other tasty prey. Close to cool, refreshing waterholes and shady clumps of acacia trees. Lots of wide-open territory—great for a new pride just starting out. Call now before this great buy is snatched up.

If they guessed lion, they're right. Now have them try a few more:

An Underground Castle: Lots of tunnels available in Mrs. Smith's backyard. Home to plenty of juicy earthworms and other tasty creatures. There's loose soil for easy tunneling and there aren't any pesky cats in the neighborhood. This super backyard buy is available immediately. (mole)

Ice Cold Ice Floes: Northern ice den now available. Great seal hunting nearby. Snow and ice everywhere. You won't find a whiter winter wonderland. Call now, before the spring thaw. (polar bear)

Now explain that each person will get a chance to write a classified ad that describes a mammal's habitat and/or home. Afterward, everyone will play a game to match classified ads to the animals that might buy them. Here's what to do:

Make a copy of pages 67, 68, and 69. Then cut out the mammal picture squares and put the pictures in a bag. Have each person pick one of the mammals, keeping the mammal's identity a secret. Then provide reference books and have the children research their mammals to find out the following information:

- where the mammal lives
- what kind of habitat the mammal lives in
- what the mammal eats
- what kind of home, if any, the mammal builds
- special facts about the mammal

Now have each person write a classified ad that describes the habitat and/or home of his or her mammal. The ad should also include information about the type of food the mammal eats and any special facts about the mammal.

When everyone is finished, pass out a blank piece of paper to each person and have everyone make a column of numbers, from 1 to 27, on the left-hand side of the page (adjust for the number in your group). Then go around the room and have each person count off. Tell the kids

to write their assigned number on the top of their ad. Also have them write their mammal's name on the ad. Then pass out copies of pages 67, 68, and 69 to each person and collect the numbered ads.

Now read each ad, one by one, and have the kids try to figure out which mammal fits each one. As you read, have the kids write the mammal's name next to the appropriate number. (Explain that some ads might fit more than one mammal and that they can write down as many mammals as they think fit the ad.)

BRANCHING OUT: HABITAT SKETCHES

Give each person a large sheet of construction paper, crayons or markers, scissors, and glue. Tell the kids to draw a picture of the habitat they described in their classified ads and then paste their mammals somewhere in the picture. They can also draw other animals that might live in the same habitat, the foods their

mammals eat, and the homes their mammals live in.

Finally, have the kids take a look at habitats and mammal homes in your area by going on an outdoor walk. For tips on what to look for, see "Mammal Safari" on page 40.

A Home in a Range

Compare home range sizes of various mammals, including those of people.

Objectives:
Define home range and territory. Explain why mammal home range sizes vary from species to species.

Ages:
Intermediate and Advanced

Materials:
- *copies of page 49*
- *pencils or pens*
- *large pieces of paper*
- *rulers*
- *chalkboard or easel paper*
- *local maps (optional)*
- *crayons or markers (optional)*

Subject:
Science

 shrew may live its entire life in an area that's smaller than a quarter of an acre. Everything it needs—food, a home, a mate, and space to raise its young—is right there. On the other hand, a grizzly bear might cover more than a hundred square miles in its lifetime to find the things it needs to survive. In this activity your kids can compare mammal home range sizes and then calculate the sizes of their own home ranges.

Begin by telling the kids that an animal's *home range* is the area it normally travels in to find food, shelter, and a mate. Within its home range, a mammal learns where the best food and water sources, escape routes, and shelters are. (Have the kids think about their own neighborhoods. They know where to get food and water, where the doctor is, where to buy clothes, and so on.)

Some mammals have areas within their home ranges called *territories*. A mammal will actively defend its territory against

competing mammals of the same species. Some mammals mark their territories with scents from their bodies. (For more about scent-marking, see "The Nose Knows" on page 8.) Some mammals also have special behaviors that say to other members of their species, "This is my territory—keep out!" If a mammal ignores a boundary and trespasses in another mammal's territory, a fight may result. (A territorial mammal usually doesn't defend its entire home range—only the area it marks as its territory. Most mammals have home ranges that overlap with those of other species.) Territories can be almost as large as the home range itself (the territory of a pride of lions), or as small as the mammal's home (a badger's burrow). A home range or territory can be occupied by a single member of a species (cougar), a male and female (dik-dik), a family (wolf pack), or a social group (prairie dog).

Now copy the following mammal names and home range sizes on a chalkboard or large piece of easel paper:

MAMMALS AND THEIR HOME RANGES (in square miles)

common shrew _____ .001

varying hare _____ .02

meadow vole
(male) _____ .0004
(female) _____ .00013

timber wolf _____ 36
(pack of 8)

grizzly bear _____ 78.5
(mother and 3 yearlings)

red fox _____ 2

raccoon _____ .02-.13

badger _____ 3.3

cougar
(male) _____ 15-30
(female) _____ 5-25

Ask if anyone can explain why the home range sizes differ. (Large animals need to eat more food than smaller animals and have to travel greater distances to find enough food; carnivores often have larger home ranges than herbivores because prey animals are sometimes more spread out than plants; animals that travel in groups require more space than solitary mammals, and so on.)

Different sexes within one species can also have different-sized home ranges. Male meadow voles and cougars both have large home ranges that overlap with the home ranges of several females of their own species. This home range overlap helps them find mates during the mating season. The females don't move around to find mates, so they have smaller home ranges.

Home range size and location may also vary with the season. For example, elk move from large summer, spring, and fall home ranges in the mountains to smaller winter home ranges in the valleys to find food. And some predators also change their home ranges from season to season to follow their prey.

WHAT'S YOUR RANGE?

In this part of the activity the kids can figure out the approximate sizes of their own home ranges and then compare their home ranges with those of other mammals.

Pass out paper and rulers and have each person draw a vertical line down the center of the page. Have them write "Things I Do" at the top of the left-hand column, and "Where I Do Them" at the top of the right-hand column. Then ask the kids to think about some of the things they do during a normal week. (go to school, visit friends at their homes, go shopping for food and clothes with parents, practice with teams after school, and so on) Have the kids write their activities in the left-hand column and then fill in where they do these things in the right-hand column across from the corresponding activity.

Now have the kids think about how far it is from their homes to each place listed on their sheets. They should write the distances they know (in miles or kilometers) next to the location. Bring in some maps of the local area so they can measure the distances they're not sure of. (You may want the children to take their lists home and have their parents help them figure out the approximate distances to each place listed.)

Next pass out a copy of page 49 to each child. Point out the circle marked "home" in the center of the page. (Explain that a wild mammal's den, resting place, lodge, or other "home" may not neccessarily be at the center of its home range, but for the purposes of this activity, we're using the center of the page as a starting point. Also point out that many mammals do not have permanent homes as people do.) Then have each person map out his or her home range by drawing in the places listed in the "Where I Do Them" column. Explain that each box on the page represents

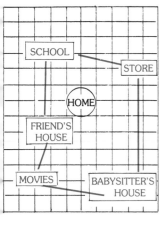

one square mile. (You can also have the children work in metrics, with each square being equal to one km^2.) For each place listed in the right-hand column of their papers, have the kids measure the correct distance and direction (north, south, east, or west) away from home, and label that spot. (Point out the scale at the bottom of the page. Explain that a half inch is equal to one mile.) For example, if one of the children lives four miles south of the school, he or she should measure the distance from his or her house two inches north and then draw and label a box to represent the school. *Note:* For children that have extremely large ranges, have them tape several grids together and then begin their mapping.

After the kids have mapped out all of their activities, have them use rulers to draw lines connecting the outermost points (see diagram). The connected lines will form the boundaries of each person's home range. To figure out the size of their home ranges, the kids should count boxes within the lines. (Some boxes won't fit completely within the lines. Tell the kids to count only the boxes that fall at least halfway within the boundaries.) The number of boxes is approximately equal to the number of square miles included in each person's home range. For example, a map of a home range covering 43 square miles would contain 43 boxes. As a follow-up, have the kids look at the list of mammals and home range sizes to see where they fit in.

Note: Younger kids can make simplified versions of home range maps. Pass out large pieces of paper and crayons or colored markers. Have the kids sketch their homes in the center of the page. Then have them draw the places they visit around their homes. When everyone is finished, share the completed maps with the group.

Tricky Tracks

Identify mammal tracks, then solve some snowy track mysteries.

Objectives:
Identify the tracks of several different types of mammals. Explain how people can use tracks to find out more about mammal habits and behaviors.

Ages:
Intermediate and Advanced

Materials:
- *copies of pages 50, 51, and 52*
- *questions on page 47*
- *reference books and field guides*
- *pencils and paper*
- *chalkboard or easel paper*
- *plaster of Paris*
- *rulers*

(continued next page)

Except for a chattering squirrel or fleeing whitetail deer, you may rarely see mammals in the wild. That's because many mammals are active only at night, and quickly take cover when people come near. But you can often find evidence that mammals have been around by looking at the tracks they leave behind in moist sand, soft soil, or snow.

And by studying these tracks, you can often figure out what these mammals were doing, where they were going, what they preyed upon, and what preyed upon them.

In the first part of this activity, your kids will learn to recognize the tracks of some common mammals. And in the second part they'll use this knowledge to answer some questions about a track-filled scene.

PART 1: WHOSE TRACK IS IT?

List the following mammals on a chalkboard or large piece of easel paper: raccoon, whitetail deer, snowshoe hare, beaver, red fox, red squirrel, black bear, house cat, muskrat, porcupine, weasel, and skunk. Then pass out a copy of page 50 to each child. Explain that each set of mammal tracks shown on the page matches one of the mammals you listed.

Tell the kids that they'll be using reference books and field guides to identify the tracks. (See page 93 for some suggestions of reference books you can use.) But before the kids begin their research, use the information below to talk about what to look for when studying mammal tracks.
Paws or Hooves: The shape of the track can tell you if it was made by a mammal

Subject:
Science

with paws or hooves. Some pawed mammals, such as foxes and bobcats, walk on "tiptoes," so only the center pads and toes on their feet show in their prints.

Mammals with hooves, such as horses, deer, cows, and elk, are also tiptoe walkers. A hoof is like a thick toenail.

Other mammals, such as raccoons, skunks, and porcupines, walk flat-footed, forming a print of the entire paw.

Claws or No Claws: Small triangular marks in front of paws are made by claws. Raccoons, skunks, coyotes, foxes, and dogs often leave claw marks. But most cats, such as cougars, lynx, and house cats, sheathe their claws when they walk or run, leaving no claw marks.

Different Patterns: The pattern of a set of tracks can help you figure out what animal made the tracks. Some mammals that live in trees, such as squirrels, hop or bound along when they're on the ground. And as they bound, their larger hind feet land ahead of their smaller front feet. If you look carefully at the prints made by the front feet, you will see they are side by side.

The tracks of hopping mammals that live on the ground, such as rabbits and some mice, are a little different. Although the hind feet still land ahead of the front feet, the front-feet tracks are usually found one in front of the other—not side by side.

Most bounders that live on the ground, such as weasels, leave paired prints as they run. (Check field guides for more track patterns.)

Slow and Fast: Most mammals' track patterns change as their gaits change. For example, a walking skunk leaves a pattern of single prints that changes into a diagonal line of prints when it breaks into a run (see illustration).

Direction: Tracks also tell in which direction a mammal was headed. Claw marks point in the mammal's forward direction, just as your toes point in the direction you're going. If claws aren't visible in the tracks, look for soil or snow pushed back by the movement of the mammal's feet. (The soil or snow will be pushed back in the direction the mammal came from.)

Snow, Soil, and Sand: Tracks will look different depending on what type of surface the mammal was walking on. Distinct tracks with well formed claw and paw shapes will show up in mud, moist earth, and in freshly fallen, relatively shallow snow. But tracks become blurry in deep snow and don't show up well at all in hard sand and dirt.

As the kids research each of the mammals to find out about its tracks, have them write the name of the correct mammal in the blank underneath the drawing. Also have the kids take notes on where each mammal lives and what it eats. (This information will help them in Part 2 of the activity.) When everyone is done, go over the correct answers (see below).

Answers:
1—raccoon; 2—snowshoe hare; 3—porcupine; 4—house cat; 5—black bear; 6—red squirrel; 7—striped skunk; 8—beaver; 9—muskrat; 10—red fox; 11—whitetail deer; 12—weasel

claws

dog

lynx

WALKING   RUNNING   CLAWS   NO CLAWS

skunk

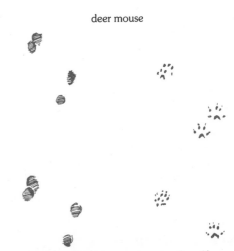

deer mouse

DEEP SNOW   WET SAND

PART 2: THE TALES TRACKS TELL

Now that they can recognize some tracks, see if your kids can "read" track clues to solve some mysteries in the snow. Copy the questions under "What Happened Here?" on a chalkboard or large piece of easel paper. Then pass out a copy of page 51 and a blank piece of paper to each person. Explain that page 51 illustrates a snow-covered scene in the northern Midwest, and the tracks of nine of the mammals that the kids identified in Part 1 appear in the scene.

The circles on the page contain close-ups of the tracks and the number beside each set of tracks corresponds to one of the questions you listed. Have the kids answer the questions to figure out the story behind each set of tracks. (They can write their answers on the blank pieces of paper.) When everyone has finished, pass out copies of page 52 and go over the kids' answers using the information we've provided in parentheses after each question. *Note:* As you discuss the page, explain that all these mammals would not be in the same area at the same time.

WHAT HAPPENED HERE?

1. Why do these tracks end at the tree? (A porcupine climbed the tree.)
2. What mammal made these tracks? (house cat)
3. Why do these tracks stop so suddenly? (A large hawk swooped down, grabbed the red squirrel, and then flew off to eat it.)
4. What mammal made these tracks and what could it have been looking for? (A raccoon crossed the creek twice looking for food.)
5. Why do these two sets of tracks both go to the brushpile, then separate and go in different directions? (A fox followed the trail of a snowshoe hare to the brushpile. The hare hid inside while the fox circled around. Finally the fox wandered off, and when the coast was clear, the hare hopped away unharmed.)
6. Why do these tracks cluster near this bush? (A deer was browsing on its twigs.)
7. What mammal came out of its den here and headed away from the creek? (black bear)
8. Why did one of these mammals stop and turn around so suddenly? (A person turned around and ran when he saw a skunk—and then tripped over a fallen branch!)

BRANCHING OUT: TAKING TRACKS HOME

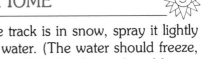

Take your group on a track walk to see if they can discover which mammals have been out and about. Muddy stream banks, sandy spots, and areas with freshly fallen snow are good places to look for tracks. Bring a ruler to measure the tracks and a field guide to help with identification.

If you find well formed prints, the kids can make plaster casts of the tracks to take home. Here's how to do it:

1. Mix the plaster with water according to the directions. (The mixture should be of about the same consistency as pancake batter.)
2. If the track is in snow, spray it lightly with water. (The water should freeze, which will harden the track and form a better cast.)
3. Make a frame around the track by placing a can or circle of cardboard around it (see illustration).
4. Pour the plaster into the frame until the surface is completely covered.
5. When the plaster has hardened, remove the frame. You might want to have the kids paint the track so it will stand out against the "frame" of the plaster surrounding it.

pour plaster

frame

paint this part of cast

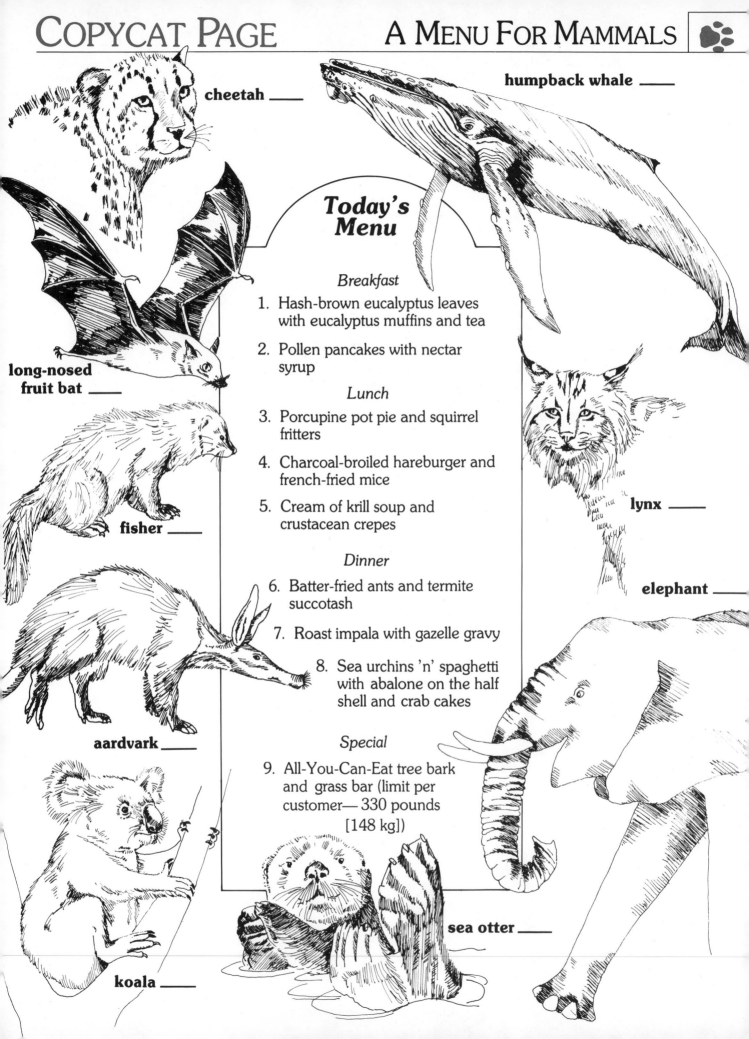

cheetah ____

humpback whale ____

long-nosed
fruit bat ____

fisher ____

aardvark ____

koala ____

lynx ____

elephant ____

sea otter ____

Today's Menu

Breakfast

1. Hash-brown eucalyptus leaves with eucalyptus muffins and tea

2. Pollen pancakes with nectar syrup

Lunch

3. Porcupine pot pie and squirrel fritters

4. Charcoal-broiled hareburger and french-fried mice

5. Cream of krill soup and crustacean crepes

Dinner

6. Batter-fried ants and termite succotash

7. Roast impala with gazelle gravy

8. Sea urchins 'n' spaghetti with abalone on the half shell and crab cakes

Special

9. All-You-Can-Eat tree bark and grass bar (limit per customer— 330 pounds [148 kg])

A HOME IN A RANGE

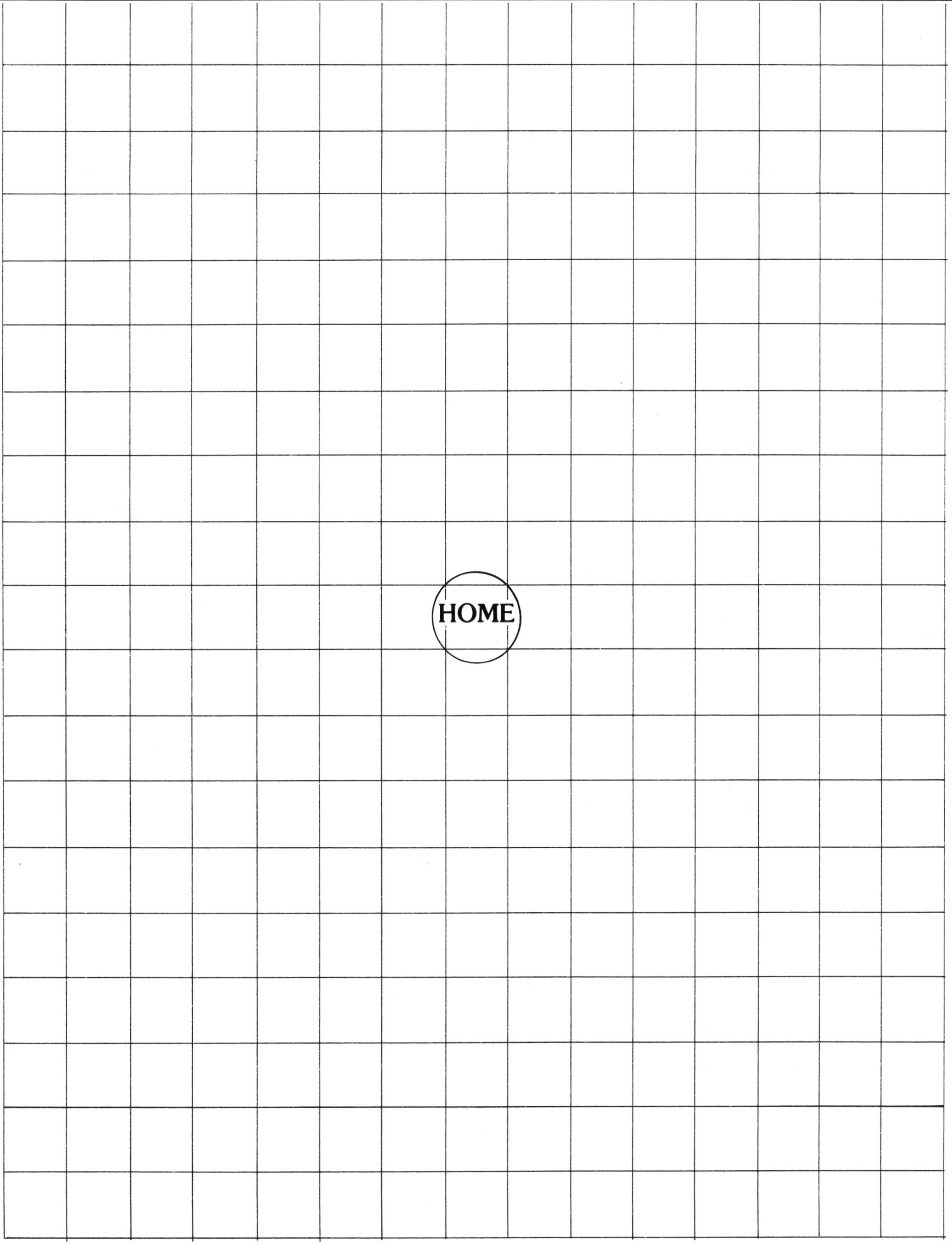

HOME

SCALE : ½ INCH = 1 MILE

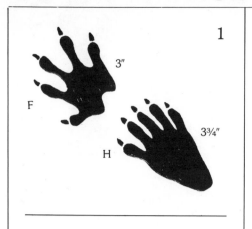

1

F
H

3"
3¾"

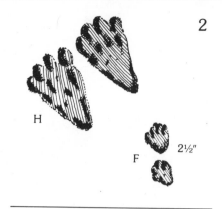

2

H
F

2½"

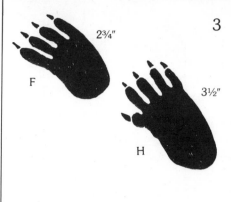

3

F
H

2¾"
3½"

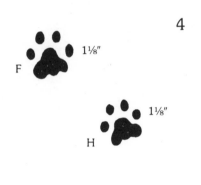

4

F
H

1⅛"
1⅛"

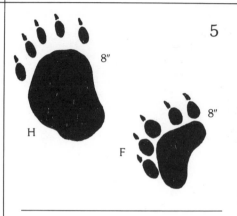

5

H
F

8"
8"

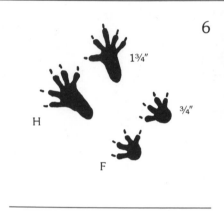

6

H
F

1¾"
¾"

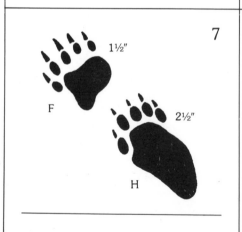

7

F
H

1½"
2½"

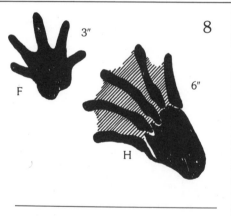

8

F
H

3"
6"

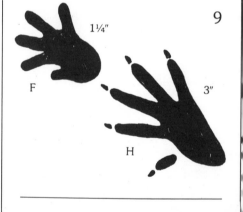

9

F
H

1¼"
3"

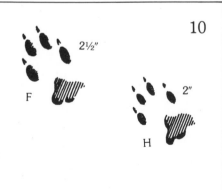

10

F
H

2½"
2"

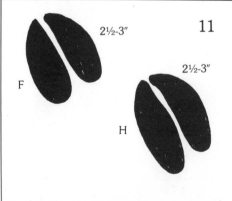

11

F
H

2½-3"
2½-3"

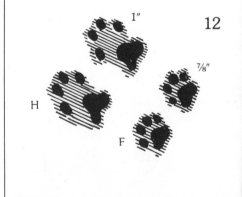

12

H
F

1"
⅞"

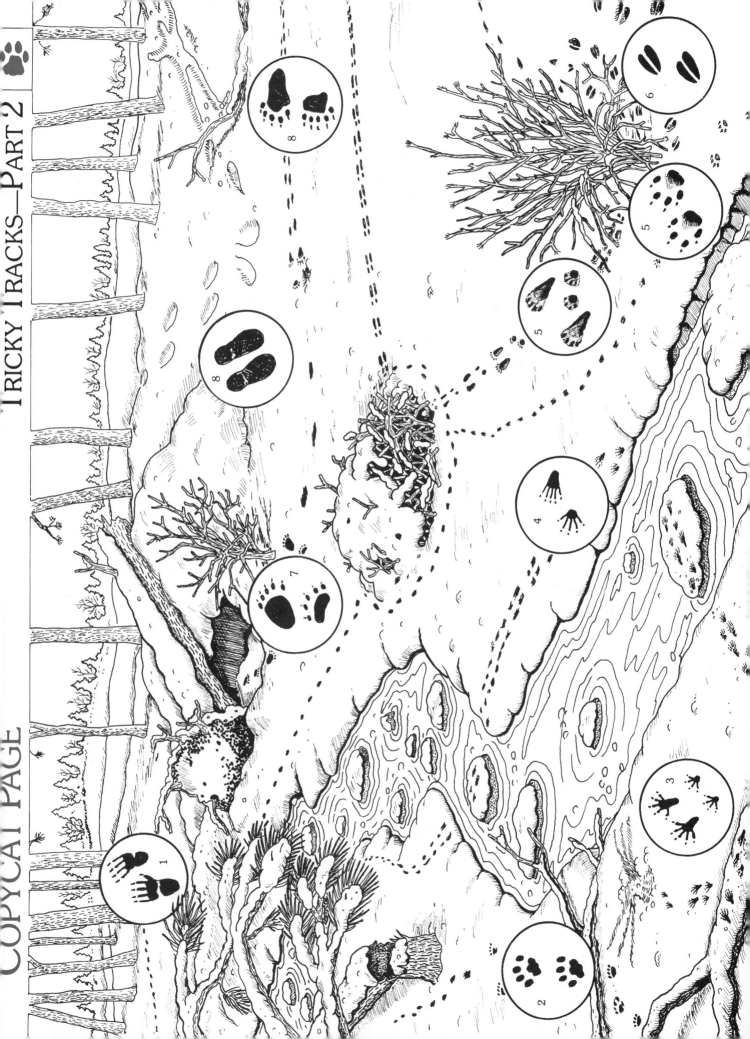

MAMMALS IN OUR LIVES

High in the Andes Mountains, camel-like animals called vicuñas are making a comeback. Prized for their soft coats of cinnamon-colored wool, vicuñas have been sought for hundreds of years—first by the Incas that originally inhabited this region, and later by the Europeans that invaded the area in the 1500s. The Incas captured the vicuñas, sheared them like sheep, and then let them go unharmed. The Europeans, however, killed the vicuñas to harvest their hides.

By 1968, after five centuries of harvest, only 10,000 vicuñas remained of an estimated original population of several million. But in 1969, the governments of Peru, Bolivia, and Ecuador signed an agreement protecting vicuñas. And today the population of these beautiful mammals is increasing, with more than 125,000 roaming the rocky reaches of western South America.

Africa's black rhinoceros faces a much grimmer future. Even though the rhino is protected by law, poachers kill these huge mammals for their horns. On the market, these horns may bring in several thousand dollars per pound. In Hong Kong, Singapore, and other areas of the Far East, powdered rhino horn is used to cure some types of illnesses, and in some parts of India it is used as an aphrodisiac. In North Yemen, a small country in the Near East, the horns are made into belts, cups, buttons, handles for ceremonial daggers, and other products. During the past 15 years, poachers have reduced the number of black rhinos drastically. Some scientists estimate that less than 3000 rhinos are alive today. Many people fear that extinction is inevitable.

In this chapter we'll look at many ways people have used—and abused—mammals throughout history. We'll also look at some of the problems mammals are facing today and how some of these problems can be solved.

MAMMALS—WE CAN'T LIVE WITHOUT THEM

Mammals have always been important to people. Our early ancestors, living tens of thousands of years ago, hunted mammoths, antelope, and horses for food. These mammals also supplied hides for clothing and shelter, tusks for weapons and tools, and inspiration for cave art and religious ceremonies.

Eventually people learned how to tame mammals. The first domestic mammals were probably dogs—descended from wolves that had become used to living near humans. People used dogs to help them hunt and to supply them with meat. Later people tamed other mammals that could supply them with meat, as well as milk, clothing, and transportation. After sheep and cattle were domesticated (about 8000 to 11,000 years ago), yaks, reindeer, pigs, horses, goats, camels, donkeys, llamas, and other mammals followed. By keeping herds of domestic mammals, people no longer had to hunt each time they needed meat or products made from these mammals.

Today we still use mammals in many ways. We eat their meat, drink their milk, make shoes and belts from their hides, fashion clothing from their fur, make pets of them, and use them in scientific and medical research. We also now understand that many mammal populations are complex and often fragile—something that has taken us thousands of years to realize.

(continued next page)

WILD MAMMALS IN DANGER

Changing temperatures, volcanic eruptions, competition from other species, and other natural happenings have caused many mammals to become extinct during the last 200 million years. But after people evolved, mammal extinctions increased dramatically. Some scientists think primitive people had a hand in wiping out cave bears, woolly mammoths, and other ice-age mammals. And the trend has continued so much that in the last 400 years about 150 species and subspecies of mammals have become extinct specifically because of people's actions—not from natural causes. Here are some of the main reasons that many mammals are in trouble today:

Shrinking Habitat: Loss of wetlands, savannahs, rain forests, deserts, forests, grasslands, and other habitats around the world is the most serious threat to mammal populations today. As millions of acres of wildlife habitat are converted into housing developments, shopping centers, roads, schools, offices, farms, and recreation areas, many mammals find it impossible to find the food, shelter, water, and space they need to survive.

Unregulated Harvest: In the past, commercial harvests have threatened many mammal populations, including those of whales, elephants, tigers, rhinoceroses, sea otters, and koalas. In some instances overhunting has caused the extinction of species, such as Steller's sea cow—a marine mammal that once lived along the coasts of the Commander Islands in the Bering Sea. These large sea mammals were killed for their tasty meat and became extinct in 1768—only 27 years after they were discovered.

Today most countries have passed strict hunting regulations to limit the number of mammals that can be killed legally. (In some instances, regulated harvests help maintain healthy populations, especially in cases where people have killed off natural predators and altered habitats. For example, if left unchecked, whitetail deer populations in many areas increase so dramatically that their food supplies are depleted. As a result, many deer die of starvation.) Most countries also prohibit the taking of rare, threatened, or endangered mammals.

Poaching: Poaching has been a problem in the past and continues to be a major problem today. Poachers kill, seriously injure, or capture protected wild mammals and sell them, or parts of them, to buyers who will pay high prices for the contraband. For example, cheetahs and other large cats are slain for their pelts, which are used to make rugs, coats, and wall hangings; chimpanzee hands are cut off and sold as ashtrays; elephants are shot for their ivory; and chimpanzees, orangutans, marmosets, and many other mammals are captured in the wild and sold illegally to zoos, animal parks, and pet stores around the world. As long as there is an illegal market for rare and threatened mammals and mammal products, poachers will continue to stay in business.

Poisons and Insecticides: People have used poisons to kill many mammals, such as rats, prairie dogs, and other rodents. Sometimes the poison also kills the animals that feed on these mammals.

Insecticides can also affect mammal populations. Some insect-eating mammals, such as some species of bats, are very sensitive to insect poison.

Introducing Non-native Animals: The introduction of dogs, cats, pigs, goats, rabbits, and other animals to places such as Australia, Cuba, and Hawaii has harmed many of the native mammal populations. For example, the introduction of exotic placental mammals into Australia has harmed some of its native marsupial populations. That's because many of these placental mammals outcompeted their marsupial counterparts. For instance, some mammalogists think that non-native wild dogs competed with Tasmanian devils (badgerlike marsupials) for food, and eventually eliminated these marsupial predators from Australia's mainland. (Tasmanian devils still roam the island of Tasmania off Australia's southern coast.)

HOPE FOR THE FUTURE

Because of the serious problems wild mammals face today, many people are working hard to protect them. Many zoos, universities, and government agencies are involved with captive breeding programs—capturing endangered wild animals, breeding them in captivity, and then releasing the offspring back into the wild. Many people hope captive breeding programs will eventually help restore rare mammal populations. But more importantly, many organizations, such as the National Wildlife Federation, The Nature Conservancy, the World Wildlife Fund, the National Audubon Society, and others, are working to protect or restore habitats around the world and are supporting research to find out more about what mammals need to survive in their natural habitats. Many of these conservation organizations are also actively involved in legislation dealing with the protection of wild mammals—making sure current laws are carried out and working to pass new legislation as needed to protect habitats and mammals that are in trouble.

Private citizens are also helping mammals by supporting conservation organizations, writing letters to let elected officials know how they feel about mammal-related legislation and issues, and getting involved in local habitat-saving projects.

Mammal Picture Stories

Create picture stories of mammals in people's everyday lives.

Objectives:
Describe several ways mammals affect people's lives. Talk about at least one way that mammals were important to prehistoric people. Describe a "mammal experience."

Ages:
Primary

Materials:
- *large pieces of drawing paper*
- *crayons, markers, and/or paints*
- *pictures of prehistoric mammal art (optional)*

Subjects:
Science, Art, and Social Studies

Here's an artistic way to reinforce the idea that mammals are a part of people's everyday lives. Start by reviewing the general characteristics of mammals (see pages 3-5). Then talk about the fact that most of us come into contact with non-human mammals every day of our lives. Ask the kids if they've seen any mammals (besides other people) that day. For example, someone might say that he or she saw the family dog or cat that morning. Another person might remember a squirrel that he or she saw on the way to school.

Also talk about the fact that people use mammals in a lot of different ways every day. Ask the kids if they can name some of these uses. (food, clothing, labor, companionship, and so on)

Next explain that mammals have always been a part of people's everyday lives. Today there's still evidence of the ways mammals affected the lives of people who lived thousands of years ago. For example, many caves—once the homes of prehistoric people—still have ancient paintings on their walls of mammals and other animals that were important to prehistoric people. Some of the paintings seem to tell the story of a hunt or other important events. (If possible, show the kids some pictures of prehistoric art.)

Now pass out large pieces of drawing paper and tell the kids that they'll be drawing their own mammal pictures. Each person's picture should tell a story about a mammal (or mammals) that he or she has come into contact with or that plays a role in his or her life. Here are some suggestions for some "mammal experiences" the kids could draw:

- a funny thing a pet dog, cat, or other mammal has done
- mammals seen on a trip to a zoo
- mammals seen on a trip to a farm
- a mammal (other than a pet) seen in the yard and the things it was doing
- a wild mammal seen on a camping trip or nature walk and the things it was doing
- several different mammals that play an important part in people's everyday lives and/or the ways we use them (pets for companionship, cows for milk, sheep for wool, and so on)

(You might want to suggest to the kids that they use a marker to draw dividing lines on their pieces of paper so that they can draw several different pictures. Together, all of the pictures should make up a mammal story.)

When the kids finish drawing, have them come up one at a time and show their drawings as they tell about their mammal experiences. Or—just for fun—you might want to have the kids exchange drawings before each person explains his or her creation. Then have the kids pretend to be archaeologists in the distant future who have just found the drawings. Each archaeologist must try to explain what each drawing might have meant to the person who drew it thousands of years ago. After each explanation, have the artist tell whether the archaeologist's interpretation was correct.

HERD OF HARTEBEESTS
PREHISTORIC ART FROM TANZANIA

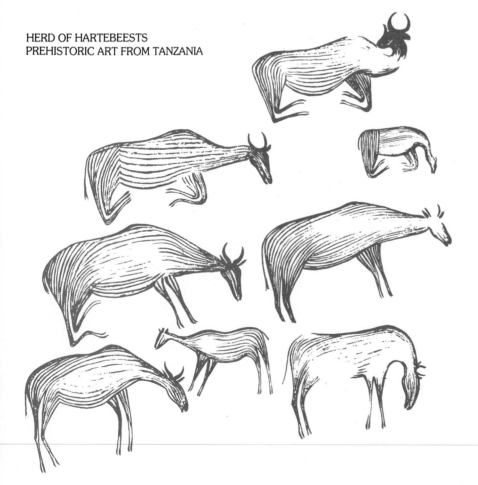

Mix 'n' Match Mammals

From tiny shrews to mighty whales, mammals come in many shapes and sizes. Try these three activities with your group to help them learn more about the characteristics of different kinds of mammals. They'll also be able to compare how the mammals are alike and how they're different. Each activity uses the mammal pictures on pages 67, 68, and 69.

PART 1: MAMMAL MINGLE

Make a copy of pages 67, 68, and 69. Then cut out the mammal squares, put them in a bag, and have each child pick one. Explain that each person has a different mammal and that everyone must research his or her mammal to try to find out the following information:
- what it eats
- what eats it, if anything
- where it lives
- how it is or has been important to people (for food, clothing, or transportation; in research; as a carrier of disease; as a pet; and so on)
- how it has influenced people (in art, music, literature, and so on)
- any special behaviors or physical characteristics it has
- what its family life is like
- whether it's endangered or threatened
- what mammals it is related to, if any

Tell the children to take notes as they research their mammals.

After everyone is finished with the research, pass out sheets of construction paper and yarn and put out a couple of paper punches where the kids can get to them. Have each person glue his or her mammal picture to the center of the page and then punch two holes in the top, about four inches (10 cm) apart. Then have the kids thread yarn through the holes so they can wear their mammal pictures around their necks.

Now pass out copies of page 66. Explain that each person must mingle with the "other mammals" to find a mammal that fits each description on the page. They can ask each other questions about their respective mammals and can use their notes to answer questions. When they find a mammal match, they should write the name of the mammal in the blank. (Explain that they can use each mammal only once.) Set a time limit and see how many children can fill in all the blanks. Then discuss each item on the page and compare results.

(continued next page)

black bear cub

PART 2: MAMMAL BINGO

Pass out a copy of pages 67, 68, and 69 to each person. Also pass out a handful of dried beans, a piece of 8½ × 11" cardboard, scissors, glue, and a piece of blank paper. Then have each person make up a mammal bingo card by cutting apart the mammal picture squares and gluing nine of them in a new arrangement on his or her piece of cardboard. Tell the children they can pick any nine of the mammals shown.

As the children are making their bingo game cards, make a list of mammal statements to use in the game. As you read a statement, the children will have to look at their cards to see if the statement matches any of the mammals pictured. If they have a match, they should place a bean on the picture that fits. And on a separate sheet of paper they should write down which mammal they marked for that particular statement. For example, if your first statement is, "a mammal that is related to dogs and lives in Australia," the kids could put a bean on the picture of the dingo—if they happened to glue that picture to their cards. Then they would write the number of the statement (#1, in this case) and the word, "dingo." Later, when someone yells "bingo," you can

check the answers by asking the winner which mammals he or she had for each statement. (Keep in mind that the kids won't have an answer for every statement. They should indicate this on their separate sheets by simply leaving a blank after the number for a particular statement. If the person who yells "bingo" doesn't have an answer for a particular statement, ask if anyone does. Then discuss the mammals the kids picked, deciding with the group whether or not each mammal is a good choice.)

Some statements might have more than one match. For example, for the statement "a mammal that is in the same mammal group as humans," the answer could be a spider monkey or an orangutan. And "a mammal herbivore" could match with the llama, camel, horse, bison, cottontail rabbit, rat, and elephant.

You can allow either one match per statement or as many matches as the children can find. The first person to fill up the sheet wins. (You can also have the children make up two or three different mammal cards and play all of them at once, or you can have them alternate cards from game to game.)

PART 3: THE SAME GAME

Pass out a copy of pages 67, 68, and 69 to each person. Also pass out large sheets of easel paper, markers, and glue. Have the children cut out the picture squares, then try to find mammals that are alike in some way. (For example, some mammals have similar habits or behaviors or similar physical characteristics, some live in the same type of habitat, some eat the same foods, and so on.) As they find matches, have them glue the mammals that are alike on a row and then write what they have in common at the far side. Here are some examples of matches:

- Blue whales, dolphins, and walruses all live in or near the ocean.
- Kangaroos and cottontail rabbits are both great hoppers.
- Leopards, dingoes, and grizzly bears are all predators.
- Kangaroos and Tasmanian devils are both marsupials.
- Vampire bats and flying squirrels are both nocturnal.

To help the children group their mammals, provide reference books for them to use. After everyone has finished, discuss the mammal matches.

OTHER WAYS TO USE THE PICTURE PAGES

- Have the kids make up mammal poems to go along with some of the mammal pictures.
- Take a trip to a zoo and have the kids try to find each mammal that's pictured.
- Have the kids build mammal mobiles using the pictures.
- Give each person one of the pictures and have him or her research how it has influenced people or how people have influenced it. Then have the kids glue their pictures on large sheets of paper and draw pictures to show what they found out.
- Make mammal books by having the children glue a different picture on each page and writing facts about each mammal underneath its picture.
- Have the kids divide up into pairs and try to think of three adjectives to describe each mammal. Go around the room to compare adjectives or keep score, giving 10 points for each unique adjective.

Mammals, Mammals, Everywhere

Take part in a mammal scavenger hunt and make a mammal mural.

Objective:
Describe several ways that mammals are important in our lives.

Ages:
Intermediate

Materials:
- *copies of clues on pages 59 and 60*
- *magazines and newspapers*
- *crayons or markers*
- *easel paper*
- *scissors*
- *glue*

Subjects:
Social Studies and Science

Mammals are everywhere in our society. Just look around. Many of our pets are mammals. Much of the food we eat comes from mammals. Some of the clothes we wear are made from mammals. And much of our art, literature, and music focuses on certain mammals.

In this activity your group will get a chance to search for ways mammals influence our lives by taking part in a mammal scavenger hunt. Afterward, they can make mammal murals from the things they found.

Before starting, review the characteristics of a mammal. (See "What Makes a Mammal a Mammal?" on pages 3-5.) Then divide the group into four or five teams and pass out a copy of the scavenger hunt clues below to each person. Explain that each team must search for pictures in magazines and/or newspapers that fit each clue. They can also draw pictures of mammals that fit the clues. (Adapt or eliminate clues to fit the needs of your group.)

Set a time limit on the research, then have each team make a mural by gluing their mammal pictures on a large sheet of easel paper. Have them think up a title for their mural. Then go over the list of clues and compare each team's pictures.

SCAVENGER HUNT CLUES

Draw or find pictures of the following:
- 2 things people wear that are made from parts of mammals
- something that only mammals have
- 3 things people eat that come from mammals
- 2 different types of mammal homes
- something a mammal would eat
- a mammal that helps people get around
- 2 mammal pets
- 2 cartoon mammals
- a type of car that is named after a mammal
- a mammal that lives on an island
- a marine mammal
- a mammal that makes sounds that people can't hear
- a mammal you see every day
- a mammal that symbolizes something

(continued next page)

- a sports team that is named after a mammal
- a mammal that is found only on one continent
- something other than clothing or food that is made from a mammal
- a mammal your team thinks best represents your state
- a mammal that is endangered or is extinct
- a mammal that can spread diseases to people
- a mammal whose name is in the title of a song

Mammal Know-It-All

Play a team game to solve a mammal word puzzle.

Objective:
Describe several ways mammals have influenced our lives.

Ages:
Intermediate and Advanced

Materials:
- *construction or easel paper*
- *thumbtacks or push-pins*
- *bulletin board*
- *envelopes*
- *index cards*
- *markers*
- *tape*
- *chalkboard or easel paper*

Subjects:
Science and Social Studies

 ere's a fun and challenging team game to help your kids review the many ways mammals influence our lives. The game is played something like the old TV program "Concentration." Team members must correctly answer a mammal-related question and then try to solve a mammal rebus (see the examples on page 61). Here's how to make the game board and play the game.

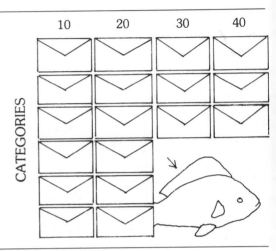

SETTING UP THE GAME BOARD

1. Tape several pieces of construction paper or easel paper together to form a large sheet about 35 × 45″ (88 × 113 cm). (The size of the paper will depend on the size of envelopes you use.)
2. Choose one of the rebuses shown here or make up your own and draw it in easy-to-read letters and pictures across the sheet. (The rebus can be a famous quote relating to mammals, a type of mammal, a famous person that studies mammals, a famous mammal saying, or anything that is mammal-related.)
3. Using thumbtacks or pushpins, attach the sheet to a bulletin board and then attach 24 envelopes in four vertical columns across the board. (There should be six envelopes in each column. See diagram.) The rows of envelopes should cover the entire rebus. (You can use standard envelopes or make your own using colored construction paper.)
4. Write each of these numbers—10, 20, 30, and 40—on a square of construction paper. Then tack the numbers, in order, above the columns of envelopes (see diagram). These numbers indicate the point values for the questions in each column.
5. Write each of these categories on a piece of construction paper and tack to the left side of each row:
   —Mammal Pets
   —Famous Mammals
   —Mammals Around the World
   —Mammals in Art, Music, Language, and Literature
   —Endangered Mammals
   —Mammals in History
6. Now copy each question listed at the end of this activity (we've included two sample sets) on an index card and insert the cards in the appropriate envelopes. (You should also write the answers on the front of each card.) The questions in each row should get progressively harder, with the ones in the 40-point column being the toughest.

Note: Adjust the questions and categories to fit the needs of your group.

HOW TO PLAY

Divide your group in half and have each team choose a captain (or appoint one). Roll dice, draw straws, or spin a spinner to see who goes first. Explain that a message about mammals is hidden under the envelopes on the game board. (Make sure everyone understands what a rebus is by drawing a simple example on a chalkboard or large sheet of easel paper.)

Point out the different categories and point values and explain that the team with the most points at the end of the game wins. Also mention that there is a 100-point bonus for correctly solving the rebus. (The game is over when a team correctly solves the rebus.)

To play, have one person on the first team pick a question. (For example, he or she might say, "Mammals in History for 40 points.") Read the question to the team and give them one minute to come up with an answer. Only the team captain can officially answer, but he or she should first confer with the whole team. If the team answers the question correctly, they get the point value of the question. Then remove the envelope that contained the question, exposing part of the rebus underneath. Let the team try to guess the mystery message.

If a team misses the question, they don't score any points and the question goes back into the envelope for another try. Then it's the other team's turn. A team can try to guess the rebus only after its captain has answered a question correctly and that envelope has been removed from the board. (When a team misses a true/false question, remove the envelope, but do not give the other team a chance to guess the message. They must first answer another question correctly before guessing.)

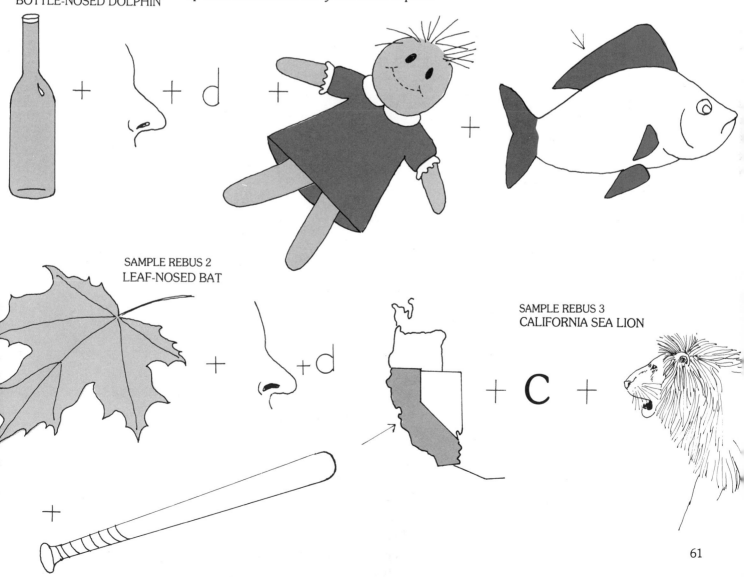

SAMPLE REBUS 1
BOTTLE-NOSED DOLPHIN

SAMPLE REBUS 2
LEAF-NOSED BAT

SAMPLE REBUS 3
CALIFORNIA SEA LION

SET 1

Mammal Pets

10: What mammal pet has a split upper lip, often eats garden vegetables, and can weigh up to 15 pounds (7 kg)? (rabbit)
20: What mammal is the most common pet in the United States? (cat)
30: What mammal was probably the first tamed for a pet? (dog)
40: What mammal pet is native to Asia, lives in the desert, and doesn't need to drink water? (gerbil)

Famous Mammals

10: Name a famous mammal that has appeared in a book. (Black Beauty, Lassie, Old Yeller, Big Red, Moby Dick, and so on)
20: What famous cartoon mammal is over 50 years old and is related to a beaver? (Mickey Mouse)
30: What famous masked mammal lives in Deep Green Wood and helps protect our environment? (Ranger Rick)
40: What famous TV star is related to a wild boar and has a best friend that is an amphibian? (Miss Piggy)

Mammals Around the World

10: What Australian mammal is the mascot for an Australian airline and feeds only on eucalyptus leaves? (koala)
20: What African mammal weighs up to 14,000 pounds (6300 kg), lives on grassy plains, has huge incisors, and makes a loud trumpeting sound when in danger? (African elephant)
30: What South American mammal has a name that begins with a double consonant and is related to camels? (llama)
40: What mammal, found in Europe, is covered with sharp spines and rolls up into a tight ball to defend itself? *Hint:* This mammal was used in the croquet game in *Alice in Wonderland.* (hedgehog)

Mammals in Art, Music, Language, and Literature

10: What mythical mammal looks like a horse but has one twisted horn on its head? (unicorn)
20: Think up a phrase or saying that is about mammals. (blind as a bat, eat like a pig, quiet as a mouse, and so on)
30: Name a song or a musical group that is named after a mammal or has something to do with mammals. ("Bingo," "Old MacDonald Had a Farm," "Mary Had a Little Lamb," The Monkees, Stray Cats, and so on)
40: Name a poem, nursery rhyme, or story that has something to do with mammals. ("Hey Diddle Diddle," "I Went to the Animal Fair," "The Cat in the Hat," and so on)

Endangered Mammals

10: True or False: Congress has passed a law that helps protect endangered species. (True—the Endangered Species Act)
20: What are two reasons that some mammals become endangered? (loss of habitat, poisoning, commercial hunting, poaching, and so on)
30: Name an endangered mammal that lives in the ocean. (humpback whale, gray whale, manatee, and so on)
40: Name two mammals in North America that are threatened or endangered. (gray wolf, grizzly bear, black-footed ferret, Delmarva fox squirrel, Florida panther, and so on)

Mammals in History

10: Name three ways mammals have been important to people throughout history. (they've provided food, clothing, shelter, transportation, and so on)
20: Name three mammals that have helped people "get around." (horse, camel, llama, donkey, ox, elephant, sled dog, seeing-eye dog, and so on)
30: What mammal was responsible for spreading the fleas that carried the Bubonic Plague, or Black Death, throughout parts of Europe during the Middle Ages? (black rat)
40: Name three mammals that are now extinct. (saber-tooth cat, mammoth, mastodon, dire wolf, and so on)

SET II

Mammal Pets

10: Which mammal pet is called "man's best friend"? (dog)
20: Thoroughbred, Arabian, Clydesdale, and Appaloosa are breeds of what domestic mammal? (horse)
30: Which popular pet is related to these wild mammals: ocelet, lynx, and cougar? (house cat)
40: Name three wild members of the dog family. (fox, wolf, coyote, jackal, dingo, and so on)

Famous Mammals

10: What famous mammal says, "Only you can prevent forest fires." (Smokey the Bear)
20: What is the name of the hooved mammal whose rider was a masked man? (Silver)
30: What female gorilla has learned to communicate with people in sign language? (Koko)
40: Name the famous albino gorilla that now lives in a zoo in Spain. (Snowflake)

Mammals Around the World

10: What black and white hooved mammals live in herds on the African plains? (zebras)
20: What African mammals live in social groups called prides? (lions)
30: What semi-aquatic Australian mammal lays eggs? (platypus)
40: Name three types of pouched mammals that live in Australia. (kangaroo, wombat, wallaby, koala, and so on)

Mammals in Art, Music, Language, and Literature

10: What farm mammal did Little Bo-Peep lose? (sheep)
20: What mammal from *Alice in Wonderland* always complains, "I'm late, I'm late! For a very important date!" (the white rabbit)
30: What mammal most likely produced Little Miss Muffet's curds and whey? (cow)
40: What saying describes calling for help when you don't really need it? ("crying wolf")

Endangered Mammals

10: What black and white endangered mammal feeds on bamboo? (giant panda)
20: What mammal in the dog family used to live in almost every habitat and region of the world north of the equator until it was hunted and poisoned almost to extinction? (wolf)
30: What weasel-like mammal preys on prairie dogs and lives in their burrows? *Hint:* This mammal has a black mask and black feet. (black-footed ferret)
40: What endangered marine mammal migrates each year along the Pacific coast of North America? (gray whale)

Mammals in History

10: What mammal has been used for thousands of years to carry people and supplies across deserts? (camel)
20: What shaggy-furred mammal used to roam the U.S. plains in huge herds? (bison)
30: What African primate was sent into space before humans? (chimpanzee)
40: What was the first mammal to orbit the earth? (dog)

The Rare Ones

Take part in a mammal survey and make a mammal presentation.

Objectives:
Name several mammals that are in trouble and describe some of the problems they're facing. Discuss several ways that people can help protect wild mammals. Graph the results of a mammal survey.

Ages:
Intermediate and Advanced

Materials:
- *copies of page 70*
- *scissors*
- *small paper bags*
- *reference books*
- *art supplies*
- *chalkboard or easel paper*

Subjects:
Science and Math

In many parts of the world, mammals are in trouble. Like other animals, they are losing their habitats as people take over more and more land for housing developments, farms, cattle ranches, and so on. And many mammals are victims of other problems as well, such as poaching, poisoning, and the selling of illegal pets. In this activity your kids can explore some of the problems mammals face by taking part in a mammal survey and by giving presentations about some mammals that are in trouble.

Pass out copies of the survey on page 70 and explain that each question has to do with a mammal that is or has been endangered or threatened. Tell the kids that they should try to answer the questions as best they can, and make it clear to them that the survey is not a test. Tell them they don't need to sign their names on the survey. (Later

they will take the same survey again and compare the answers from both.)

As the kids are filling out the survey, write each of these mammal names on a slip of paper and put them into a bag:

- African elephant
- bison
- black-footed ferret
- black rhinoceros
- Florida panther
- golden lion tamarin (also called golden marmoset)
- grizzly bear
- humpback whale
- jaguar
- panda
- mountain gorilla
- orangutan
- Tasmanian devil
- vicuña

vicuña

Leonard Lee Rue III

63

After the kids have finished answering the survey questions, have them cut out their answers along the solid black lines. (They should have 15 cut-out answers.) Collect their answers, one question at a time, and put all of the answers for each question into a separate bag. Label each bag "pretest" and also write the number of the question on the front of the bag. (For example, the first bag would be labeled "pretest, question #1.") Tell the kids they will be tallying the results of the survey later. (See "Tallying the Survey" at the end of the activity.)

black rhinoceros

Leonard Lee Rue III

Next divide the group into teams of two or three and have each team pick one of the mammal names out of the bag. Explain that the teams should research their mammals to find out as much as they can about them. Most of the mammals are endangered species. Others, while not yet listed as endangered, are threatened by problems that could soon place them on the endangered species list. And a few of the mammals were very close to extinction in the past and have since made a comeback.

Now write the following questions on a chalkboard or large piece of easel paper to let the kids know some of the things they should try to find out:

- Where does your mammal live?
- What does your mammal eat?
- Is your mammal in trouble? If so, describe some of the problems it's facing.
- What are people doing to help your mammal survive? (If your mammal is no longer in trouble, describe what people did to help it make a comeback.)

Tell the kids that they may need to do some "digging" to find the answers to all four questions, since encyclopedias may not have all the information they'll need. Encourage them to use the *Readers' Guide to Periodical Literature* to find current magazine articles about their mammals. They may also be able to find some up-to-date information in books about endangered species. (See the bibliography on page 75 for suggestions.)

Next explain that each team will get a chance to present what they've discovered about their mammal. Here are some ideas for the kinds of things the kids could do for their presentations. (The kids can pick one or more of these ideas or come up with their own.)

- make posters showing the mammal in its habitat
- write the answers to the questions in bright colors on large sheets of easel paper and illustrate each answer
- write one or more "public service announcements" and read them to the group
- make buttons that have catchy slogans about the mammal and information about why it's in trouble
- hold a discussion about the problems the mammal faces and the ways people are helping to protect it
- draw a map showing the mammal's range
- put on a skit about the mammal
- make up a song, poem, or story about the mammal

Set a date for the presentations, giving the kids enough time to research their mammals and to decide how they want to present what they've learned. After each team gives their presentation, review the problems each mammal is facing and discuss the ways people are helping the mammal.

After all the teams have given their presentations, pass out another copy of the "Mammal Survey Questions" to each person. Have the kids fill out the survey again and cut apart the questions. Then collect the questions as before, but label each bag "post test."

TALLYING THE SURVEY

Now tell the kids they are going to tally the two surveys and graph the results. Give each person one of the bags and have him or her count up the results. (For large groups, have several children work together.) For example, the person who has the bag marked "pretest, question #1" would count how many people picked answer "a," how many picked "b," and how many picked "c."

As the kids are counting the results, draw an x and y axis for a graph on the chalkboard or large sheet of easel paper. Label the x axis "question number" and the y axis "percent correct," then mark off the increments for both axes (see diagram). Next start with question #1 and ask if anyone knows the correct answer. (See the end of this activity for answers.) Ask whoever counted up the first pretest question to tell how many people answered the question correctly. Show the children how to figure out what percentage of the group answered the question correctly. (Divide the number that answered the question correctly by the total number of people who took the survey. Then multiply this number by 100. For example, if 12 kids had the correct answer out of a group of 30, 40% would have answered it correctly.) Do the same for the first post test question and compare the results. As you tally each question, discuss it and then have each person come up and graph the results of his or her question. (You might want to make both a line and a bar graph.)

After the graph is finished, discuss the results of the survey. Ask the kids if educating each other helped them learn more about the problems mammals face. Also ask them what the number one danger to mammals is today. Explain that while problems such as oil spills, air pollution, poaching, and other problems can really threaten mammals and other animals, the biggest problem all wildlife faces is the loss of habitat. But point out that many conservation organizations are working hard to protect wild mammals, other wildlife, and wildlife habitats. (See "Hope for the Future" on page 55 for the names of some conservation organizations that your group can get involved with.)

Answers:
1—b; 2—c; 3—False; 4—b; 5—a; 6—c; 7—c; 8—a; 9—False; 10—b; 11—a; 12—b; 13—a; 14—b; 15—c

MAMMAL SURVEY RESULTS

Post Test
Pretest

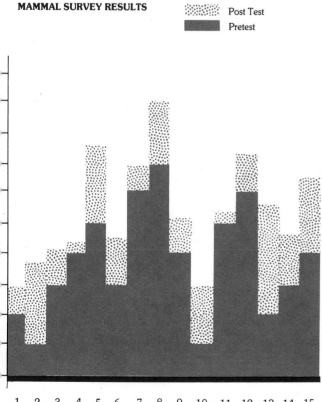

1 2 3 4 5 6 7 8 9 10 11 12 13 14 15
QUESTION NUMBER

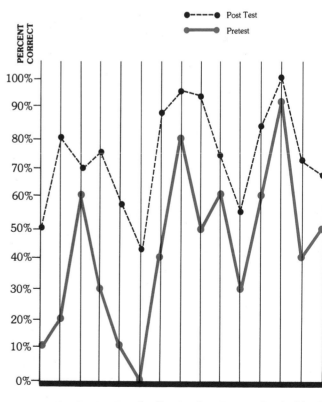

Post Test
Pretest

PERCENT CORRECT

100%
90%
80%
70%
60%
50%
40%
30%
20%
10%
0%

1 2 3 4 5 6 7 8 9 10 11 12 13 14 15
QUESTION NUMBER

Find a mammal that:

1. doesn't eat meat _____

2. lives in grassy areas _____

3. is endangered _____

4. eats only one type of food _____

5. is a fast runner _____

6. does work for people _____

7. lives in social groups _____

8. is related to humans _____

9. is related to wolves _____

10. might eat your garden vegetables _____

11. has a pouch _____

12. has a special way of protecting itself _____

13. makes an unusual sound _____

14. uses its front legs to dig _____

15. is sometimes eaten by owls and other large

    birds of prey _____

16. has been trapped for its fur _____

17. is a predator _____

18. is an herbivore _____

19. is related to pigs _____

20. migrates _____

COPYCAT PAGE

MAMMAL PICTURE PAGE

Flying Squirrel

Hedgehog

Orangutan

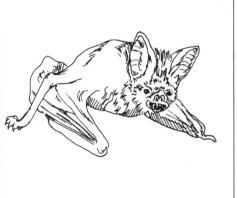

Vampire Bat

Bison

Tasmanian Devil

Rat

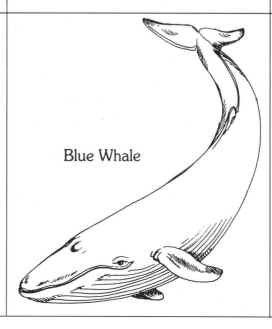

Blue Whale

Dingo

COPYCAT PAGE

MAMMAL PICTURE PAGE

Camel

Armadillo

Kangaroo

Prairie Dog

Black Rhinoceros

Dolphin

Wild Horse

Leopard

Elephant

RANGER RICK'S NATURESCOPE: AMAZING MAMMALS

MAMMAL PICTURE PAGE

Llama

Mole

Aardvark

Warthog

Cottontail Rabbit

Grizzly Bear

Walrus

Beaver

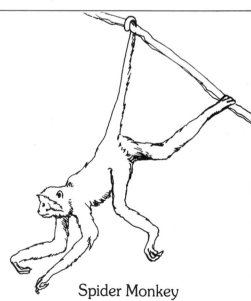

Spider Monkey

COPYCAT PAGE

THE RARE ONES

MAMMAL SURVEY QUESTIONS

1. Which of these mammals is endangered?
   a) raccoon
   b) Florida panther
   c) bison

2. Which of these mammals was once seriously endangered but has made a comeback?
   a) raccoon
   b) Florida panther
   c) bison

3. True or false: It's legal to import the spotted coat of the jaguar, a big cat that lives in South America, into the United States.

4. Which of these endangered mammals is being reintroduced into the wild?
   a) humpback whale
   b) golden lion tamarin
   c) black bear

5. What part of the black rhinoceros is in great demand in some countries?
   a) its horn
   b) its teeth
   c) its skin

6. Which of these mammals is disappearing from Yellowstone National Park?
   a) black bear
   b) bison
   c) grizzly bear

7. Which of these mammals relies on bamboo?
   a) African elephant
   b) mountain gorilla
   c) panda

8. Which of these mammals did the dingo probably wipe out (by competing for food and other resources) on the Australian mainland?
   a) Tasmanian devil
   b) red kangaroo
   c) domestic sheep

9. True or false: Poaching is no longer a threat to mountain gorillas.

10. Which of the following has not been a big threat to orangutans?
    a) destruction of its rain forest habitat
    b) oil spills
    c) over-collecting for zoos

11. Which of these problems affects sea otter populations?
    a) oil spills
    b) selling of illegal pets
    c) hunting too many otters for their meat

12. Which of the following do poachers kill elephants for?
    a) their skin
    b) their tusks
    c) their ears

13. Which of these mammals had been considered by many to be extinct until it was rediscovered in 1981 in the western United States?
    a) black-footed ferret
    b) black-tailed jackrabbit
    c) pronghorn antelope

14. Which of these mammals is sheared for its fine wool?
    a) bighorn sheep
    b) vicuña
    c) Dall's sheep

15. Which of these problems is the most serious threat to mammals today?
    a) overhunting
    b) pollution
    c) loss of habitat

RANGER RICK'S NATURESCOPE: AMAZING MAMMALS

CRAFTY CORNER

Mammal Magnets

Make mammal-shaped dough magnets.

Ages:
Primary and Intermediate

Materials:
- *baking soda*
- *cornstarch*
- *cold water*
- *saucepan*
- *stove*
- *spoon*
- *plastic bag*
- *plate*
- *damp towel*
- *small, mammal-shaped cookie cutters (optional)*
- *wax paper*
- *acrylic paints, watercolors, or markers*
- *clear nail polish or acrylic sealer (optional)*
- *paint brushes*
- *glue*
- *small magnets*
- *reference books (optional)*

Subjects:
Arts and Crafts

Follow these easy steps to make colorful mammal magnets:

1. Flatten a golf ball-sized lump of dough (*see recipe below*) onto a piece of wax paper using the palm of your hand. The pressed dough should be *at least ¼ inch (6 mm) thick.* (Don't press it too thin or else the dough may break as it dries.)
2. Mold the dough into the shape of a mammal, using pictures of mammals for reference. (Younger children can use cookie cutters to cut out mammal shapes.)
3. Make eyes, a nose, ears, spots, or other features by adding tiny bits of dough or by carving them into the dough with a pencil point. (Be careful not to push the pencil point in too deeply or the dough may break as it dries. Also avoid adding long, thin tails, horns, legs, or other features that may break easily.)
4. Let dry overnight.
5. Carefully remove the mammal shape from the wax paper and paint it with acrylic paints or watercolors or color it with markers. Let dry. (Once your mammal is dry, you might want to paint on a layer of clear nail polish or acrylic sealer. [Acrylic sealer is available at most craft stores.] This extra layer will protect your creation and make it shine.)
6. Glue a small magnet on the back of the mammal. (You can get small magnets at some electronic and craft stores.) Large mammals may need two magnets.

HOW TO MAKE CRAFT DOUGH

This recipe will make enough dough for at least 20 magnets.

- 4 cups baking soda
- 2 cups cornstarch
- 2½ cups cold water

Mix all of the ingredients in a medium-sized saucepan and cook over medium heat, stirring constantly. Cook about 10 minutes or so, until the mixture is the consistency of mashed potatoes. Remove from heat, turn out onto a plate, and then cover with a damp cloth. After the dough cools, knead it gently into a smooth ball. Then store it in a tightly sealed plastic bag and refrigerate until you're ready to use it.

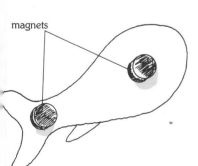

magnets

Mammal Greetings

Make mammal cards to write messages in.

Ages:
Intermediate

Materials:
- *construction paper*
- *glue*
- *crayons or markers*
- *scissors*
- *pencils*
- *cotton balls and fabric scraps (optional)*
- *reference books or magazines (optional)*

Subjects:
Arts and Crafts

Your kids can create their own mammal note cards to send to their friends. Just pass out a piece of construction paper to each child and then have the kids follow these directions:

1. To make the construction paper sturdier, fold it in half and glue the halves together. (Remind the kids to spread the glue evenly.) Let dry.
2. Fold the paper in half again to form a card.
3. Use a pencil to draw the outline of a mammal on the construction paper. (You may want to bring in magazines or books with mammal pictures to help the kids choose a mammal.) Draw the mammal so that its back lies along the fold of the card (see diagram).
4. Cut the card out along the outline. (Be sure to hold the two layers of paper together while cutting. And don't cut through the fold at the top of the card!)
5. Draw in eyes, stripes, and other details with crayons or markers, or glue down pieces of colored construction paper for these features. You might also want to use cotton, fabric, or other materials for tails, fur, and so on.
6. Write a special message or poem inside the card, then send it to someone special!

APPLYING YOUR KNOWLEDGE
Questions, Questions, and More Questions

1. Mammals are one major group of vertebrates. What are the four others? (fish, reptiles, birds, amphibians)
2. True or false: Mammals are the only animals that are warm-blooded. (False. Birds are also warm-blooded.)
3. Mammals evolved from which group of vertebrates? (reptiles)
4. True or false: Mammals are the only animals that nurse their young. (True)
5. What are the three basic kinds of mammal teeth? (incisors or front teeth, canines or eye teeth, premolars and molars or cheek teeth)
6. What is underfur? (the short, fluffy hair that's close to many mammals' skin and helps keep them warm)
7. Where is a female mammal's milk produced? (in her mammary glands)
8. Porcupine quills are a modified form of _____. (hair)
9. Dolphins, many bats, and some other mammals can find food and avoid obstacles through a special hearing system called _____. (echolocation)
10. The amount of time it takes a mammal baby to develop inside its mother's womb is called the _____ period. (gestation)
11. True or false: All mammal young are born live. (False. Most mammal mothers give birth to live young, but platypuses and echidnas lay eggs.)
12. Mammals that are born after a short gestation period and attach themselves soon after birth to their mothers' nipples (sometimes inside a pouch) are called _____. (marsupials)
13. True or false: A mammal that is active very soon after birth is called an altricial mammal. (False. It is called a precocial mammal.)
14. True or false: All baby mammals grow up in the safety of a "nursery." (False. Usually, only altricial mammals have "nurseries." Most precocial mammals make their homes out in the open.)
15. True or false: All male mammals help raise their young. (False. Most mammal fathers don't get involved in family duties at all.)
16. What are two ways mammals can avoid harsh living conditions or reduced food supplies? (migrate, hibernate or estivate, cache food, change their diets)
17. True or false: Herbivores feed on dead animals. (False. Herbivores feed on plants. Carrion eaters feed on dead animals.)
18. List three ways different mammals escape predators. (flee, fight, play dead, live in a group, smell bad, display sharp quills or other protective features)
19. What do omnivores eat? (a lot of different foods, including fresh meat, carrion, fruits, nuts, and so on)
20. Name three ways people have used mammals. (for transportation, labor, companionship, food, clothing, research, entertainment)
21. Name three reasons that some mammals have become endangered or extinct. (loss of habitat, overhunting, poaching, poisons and pesticides, competition with introduced species, natural catastrophes)
22. Which of the following mammals is not listed as endangered or threatened in the lower 48 states: the black-footed ferret, gray wolf, black bear, or sea otter? (black bear)
23. What are two ways people are helping endangered mammals? (passing laws to protect them and their habitats, establishing and maintaining captive breeding programs, banning products made from endangered mammals, and so on)

Glossary

adaptation—a behavior, physical feature, or other characteristic that helps an animal survive and make the most of its habitat. For example, a giraffe's long neck helps this mammal reach leaves high in the trees. This helps it avoid competition from other leaf-eating animals that can't reach as high.

altricial—the condition in which an animal is born helpless and often hairless and blind. Humans, wolves, and many other mammals have altricial young.

browser—an animal that eats the leaves, shoots, or bark of trees and shrubs. Deer, giraffes, and koalas are examples of mammals that browse.

canines—side teeth used for piercing and grasping. Also called eye teeth.

carnivore—an animal that eats meat. Wolves, lions, and polar bears are examples of carnivores.

carrion—the remains of dead animals. Hyenas, jackals, and many other mammals eat a lot of carrion.

cerebral cortex—the area of the brain where learning takes place. This area is more developed in mammals than in other animal groups.

cranium—the hard case of bone or cartilage that surrounds the brain.

diaphragm—the muscle that separates the chest from the abdomen and aids in breathing. Mammals are the only animals that have diaphragms.

echolocation—a special hearing system in which an animal produces short, high-pitched sounds and then listens for the echoes the sounds make when they bounce off of objects around them. Bats and dolphins are examples of mammals that *echolocate*.

estivation—a deep "sleep" some animals enter during drought. Estivation is a hot-weather version of hibernation.

fur—a thick covering of hair on many mammals' bodies that protects and insulates them.

grazer—an animal that eats mostly grasses. Bison, kangaroos, and antelope are examples of mammals that graze.

guard hairs—the long, coarse hairs that protect a mammal's underfur and give its coat shape.

habitat—an animal's home. For example, the habitat of a zebra is an open plain.

herbivore—an animal that eats plants. Kangaroos, beavers, and pandas are examples of herbivores.

hibernation—a deep "sleep" some animals enter during the winter when food supplies are limited. A woodchuck is an example of a mammal that hibernates.

incisors—front teeth used for cutting and snipping.

insectivore—an animal that eats insects and other small invertebrates. Shrews, moles, and many bats are examples of insectivores.

mammalogy—the study of mammals. A *mammalogist* is a scientist who studies mammals.

marsupial—a mammal that gives birth to tiny, undeveloped young after a short gestation period. The young attach themselves to nipples (often inside a pouch, or pocket) soon after birth, and there they finish developing. Kangaroos, koalas, and Tasmanian devils are examples of marsupial mammals.

molars and premolars—cheek teeth used for crushing, grinding, and sometimes slicing.

monotreme—a mammal that lays eggs. The duck-billed platypus and two species of echidnas are the only monotremes.

niche—the "job" of a plant or animal in its habitat. For example, the niche of a wildebeest could be described as: daytime feeder; grazer; food for lions, cheetahs, jackals, and hyenas; and seasonal migrator.

omnivore—an animal that eats a wide range of foods—from grasses and fruits to fresh meat and carrion. Bears, raccoons, and humans are examples of omnivores.

placenta—the organ that nourishes the growing embryo inside the mother's womb. Both marsupial and placental mammals have placentas but those of placental mammals are more efficient. Most mammals are placental mammals.

precocial—the condition in which an animal is born already well developed and able to get around on its own soon after birth. All hooved mammals are precocial.

umbilical cord—a group of blood vessels that connects an embryo with the placenta and supplies oxygen and nourishment to the developing baby.

underfur—the short, fluffy fur that lies next to a mammal's skin and helps keep it warm.

uterus—the organ in a female mammal in which a baby develops. The uterus is sometimes called the *womb*.

warm-blooded—being able to maintain a constant body temperature independent of the outside temperature. All mammals are warm-blooded.

That's A Mouthful!

Match teeth to the mammal mouth where they belong

Objectives:
Learn that the number and kinds of teeth vary among mammal species. Infer that mammals have different kinds of teeth for eating different kinds of food.

Ages:
Primary

Materials:
• *Copies of page 84*
• *Scissors*
• *Glue or tape*
• *Crayons, markers*

Subject:
Science

Ask your kids how they use their teeth when they eat (to bite and cut into food; to chew food into smaller pieces that are easier to swallow and digest). Without looking in a mirror, can your kids describe or draw their teeth? Pair them up and have one smile while the other draws the teeth and vice versa.

With which teeth do kids think they cut and bite into food (the four center incisors)? Which teeth tear into food (the pointed cuspid, or canine, teeth one on each side of the incisors)? Which crush, grind, and chew food? (The premolars, or bicuspids, and the molars do. The bicuspids have two points, or cusps, while the molars have broad, flat surfaces.)

Ask kids what kinds of foods they eat and list their responses on the board. Point out that their different kinds of teeth allow them to eat both plant and animal foods. The same goes for other kinds of mammals: The number and kinds of teeth that they have enable them to eat the kinds of food they do.

Hand out copies of page 84. Invite kids to color the animal heads. Tell them to cut out the five mouths and challenge them to match the teeth to the mouth in which they belong. Kids can tape or glue the cut-out teeth in place. They can also cut out the animal heads and line them up side by side or mount them on poster board or cardboard.

Divide the class into groups and assign each group one of the animals. Ask each group to research what kinds of food its animal eats. By looking at the teeth in that animal's mouth, could the group have predicted that the animal would eat the kinds of food it does? For example, meat eaters such as the lion have large, sharp canine teeth to stab and hold prey. Plant-eating zebras lack these sharp stabbers but have incisors for clipping plants. You may wish to hand out copies of the wolf's mouth and teeth on page 20 (see Layered Wolf) for reference. Have the groups compare their animal's teeth to their own. How are they alike? How are they different?

Allow each group to present its findings to the class so that all your kids can list what that animal eats. Whenever you discuss a new mammal species, encourage kids to draw that mammal's head and teeth and add it to their collection. See if they can predict what that animal eats by looking at its teeth.

Copycat Page Answers

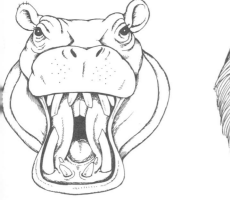

Endangered

Objectives:
Learn about four mammals that are endangered. Research other endangered mammals and find out what is being done to help save them.

Ages:
Primary and Intermediate

Materials:
- *Copy of page 87*
- *Scissors*
- *Tape or glue*
- *Crayons, markers*

Subjects:
Science, Art

What do your kids think the word "endangered" means with respect to wildlife? It means "in danger of becoming extinct" (gone forever). And not in the distant future but in the foreseeable future.

In many countries, including the United States, legislation has been passed that protects species which scientists agree are endangered. However, more and more, scientists are encouraging people to realize that many species are in danger of becoming extinct because the places in which they are best fitted or adapted to live—their habitats—are being destroyed. If this trend continues, many more species will wind up on the endangered list.

Review with your kids some of the other reasons for wildlife's being endangered. Refer to Wild Mammals in Danger on pages 54 and 55.

One way to start helping to save endangered species is to make more people aware of the problem. Hand out copies of page 87 and invite your kids to color the four endangered mammals pictured. Allow them to cut out the two rectangles and the two circles and tape them to their notebooks, wear them as badges that attract attention, or glue them onto paper or poster board and send them as cards or use them as bookmarks. Call on kids and ask them what they would tell a friend or family member who asks what the badge or sticker means.

You can also allow kids to tape or glue their cut-out mammals to the same piece of poster board and create a poster of endangered mammals. Under each picture, they should write a short story about that animal and why it is in danger. Students can research the animal or use the information on pages 76 and 77, which you can copy and hand out.

Encourage kids to find out about other endangered mammals such as cheetahs, okapis, African wild dogs, Asian elephants, Bengal tigers, etc. Allow kids to draw these animals and add them to their posters. Be sure kids find out what is being done to try to save the mammals.

ENDANGERED MAMMALS FACT SHEET

MOUNTAIN GORILLA

- lives in mountain forests in central Africa
- can weigh up to 400 pounds (182 kg)
- feeds mainly on leaves and plant shoots
- lives in groups of about 15 gorillas led by one male
- large adult male is called a silverback
- gorillas are not ferocious; male hoots and pounds his chest only when threatened
- spends most of its time on the ground but can climb
- only about 600 are alive today
- is endangered due to poachers who sell them to illegal collectors
- Farming and logging are reducing the gorillas' habitat to provide for Africa's increasing human population.

TIMBER WOLF

- is also known as the gray wolf
- lives in the northern United States, Canada, Alaska, and parts of Eurasia
- lives in forests, on mountains, and on the tundra
- dens up in hollow logs, rock cracks, or burrows
- usually hunts at night in packs of up to 20 wolves led by the most powerful male
- Close to 2 million were killed between 1850 and 1900 because farmers and ranchers settling the West feared the wolves would prey on cattle and sheep. Wolves did attack these animals because the numbers of their natural prey—deer, moose, bison—kept dropping as wild habitat was taken over for towns and farms.
- Ecologists now understand that wolves are part of the natural ecosystem. When wolves disappeared, coyotes often moved in.
- Only about 2500 wolves live in the United States, about 7000 in Alaska, and perhaps 30,000 in Canada.
- Some timber wolves have been put back into Yellowstone National Park where they once lived. The wolves are free to hunt moose and other animals that live in the park. Even so, nearby farmers are worried about their livestock.

BLACK RHINOCEROS

- lives in small parts of eastern and southern Africa
- inhabits the edge of forests and dry scrubland
- can weigh up to 3000 pounds (1363 kg)
- wallows in water or mud to cool off or to get rid of flies
- feeds mainly on twigs
- is armed with two nose horns to defend against predators such as lions and to attack other rhinos that won't leave its territory
- is overhunted for its horns that may be ground up for medicines or made into handles for daggers; also hunted for its hide or as a trophy
- Only about 3000 are alive and are still being illegally shot despite laws protecting the black rhinoceros.

STELLER'S SEA LION

- lives in waters off the west coast of Alaska, Canada, and the United States, and the east coast of Russia and Japan
- can weigh up to 2200 pounds (1000 kg)
- hunts octopus, squids, fish, and crustaceans
- can dive deep and stay underwater 20 minutes without resurfacing for air
- In spring males claim territory on rocky islands and females give birth to pups.
- About 100,000 are alive today but numbers are dropping.
- No one knows if the cause is disease, pollution, lack of enough prey to catch, drowning in fishing nets, or some other cause.

One More Time

Objectives:
Learn about how some mammals digest their food. Infer that a human's digestive system is more like that of a lion than a cow.

Ages:
Primary and Intermediate

Materials:
- *Copies of page 85*
- *Pencil or pen*
- *Crayons, markers*

Subject:
Science

Ask your kids what they think happens to the food they eat once it enters their mouths. What takes place inside their mouths? (Food is chewed with their teeth, saliva mixes with food, their tongue moves food around, food is swallowed at the back of the mouth where the throat is.) Then what happens? (Swallowed food goes into the stomach.) Do kids know what process is taking place? (Answer: digestion.)

Explain that food contains nutrients, such as sugars, starches, proteins, fats, vitamins, and minerals, that their bodies need for energy and as building blocks so they can grow and stay healthy. These nutrients in food are often too big for the body to use. But when food is broken down, or digested, the body can take in all the nutrients it needs in a form it can use. Parts of food, such as fiber, that the body cannot digest pass from one end of the digestive system to the other, where they are excreted.

Hand out copies of page 85 and challenge kids to solve the mazes. Then ask what happens to the food the lion eats. (It moves from the mouth, down the food tube or esophagus, into the stomach, and then through the intestines.) What happens to the cow's food? (It moves from the mouth, to the rumen, then back to the mouth, then to the reticulum and the omasum, then to the abomasum, and then through the intestines.)

Can kids figure out why the cow's food goes back to its mouth? (Answer: to be rechewed.)

WHAT HAPPENED?

Have kids follow along on their mazes as you explain the following:

1. Cows eat grasses and other kinds of plants. They grind these plants with their broad, flat teeth as saliva softens and moistens them.

2. When the chewed grasses reach the rumen, they are covered with bacteria that live there. These bacteria start to break open the tough parts of the grass cells. Without their help, the cow could not digest its food and release enough nutrients to stay alive. However, the bacteria cannot get the job done unless the swallowed food is rechewed. So from time to time part of the food returns to the mouth. When the rechewed food, or cud, is swallowed again, it goes to the reticulum and then the omasum.

3. In the reticulum more bacteria attack it and, in the omasum, water is squeezed out. The next stop is the abomasum.

4. In the abomasum digestion continues as stomach acids and juices attack the food.

5. Stress that the rumen, the reticulum, the omasum, and the abomasum are the four chambers that make up a cow's stomach. Of these, the abomasum is the only chamber that is like the stomach of a lion.

6. Ask kids what lions eat. (Answer: meat.) A lion's teeth pull, slice, tear, and chew food as saliva pours over it. The chewed food is swallowed and goes to the stomach.

7. In both plant eaters and meat eaters, most digestion takes place in the small intestine, where more digestive juices pour over food and break it down into simple nutrients.

8. These nutrients cross through the walls of the small intestine and into the blood. Undigested food continues along to the large intestine to be excreted.

Which digestive system do kids think is more like theirs? (Answer: the lion's.) Why? (People have only one stomach, not a four-chamber stomach.) Tell kids that humans lack the bacteria that can break down the very toughest parts of plant cells called fiber. Even so, fiber is important in a person's diet because it provides bulk that helps the intestines work smoothly.

Mammal Cave

Match pictures of mammals painted in a cave with those of prehistoric mammals that are extinct

Objectives:
Learn about mammals that lived during the great Ice Age. Infer which modern day mammals are related to prehistoric mammals depicted in cave paintings.

Ages:
Primary

Materials:
Copies of page 86
Tape, glue
Pencil
Scissors
Poster board
Crayons, markers

Subjects:
Science, Art

Can your kids imagine living in a world with no cities, no towns, no electricity, no machines, no food stores, no medicines, no houses, no school, etc? How do they think they would survive? What would they eat? Where would they find shelter?

Humans who lived in prehistoric times faced just such a challenge, especially those who lived during the great Ice Age. The great Ice Age began about 2 million years ago and lasted until about 12,000 years ago. During this time, massive sheets of glacial ice formed and spread over much of Europe, Asia, and North America. The moving ice blanketed mountains, choked rivers, filled valleys, and flattened forests. In some places the ice was 3 miles (4.8 km) thick.

At least four times during the great Ice Age the climate changed from cold to warm. In many places the ice sheets melted. But the warming did not last and the bitter cold returned with new sheets of thick ice. About 12,000 years ago the last change back to warm melted most of the ice. Today, ice sheets cover less than 10 percent of the earth's surface.

At the edge of the massive ice sheets lived large furry mammals that are now extinct. What little is known about these animals comes from fossils they left behind. Some of these fossils were discovered in caves along with cave paintings made by prehistoric people who found shelter there. Some of the oldest cave paintings, dating back to around 30,000 years ago, have been discovered in Europe. The images were painted using rocks and minerals the cave dwellers found around them. Were they drawn to show animals the cave people hunted, or feared, or held in high esteem? No one yet knows. But the paintings remain a unique record of creatures that no longer exist.

Hand out copies of page 86. Have kids imagine that they have found a cave—not just any cave but a prehistoric cave—and have joined a team of scientists to explore it for the very first time. Ask them to describe what such an adventure might be like and how they would react if they discovered animal pictures painted on the cave walls and ceiling. Invite kids to

(continued next page)

draw a line from each painted mammal on their sheets to the Ice Age mammal below that it most likely represents. Then have kids draw another line from each Ice Age mammal to its modern cousin. Which characteristic most distinguishes the Ice Age mammals from their cousins alive today? (Answer: thicker fur.) Why do kids think Ice Age animals needed such thick fur? (Answer: to survive the cold climate.)

Use the key below to have kids label each of the animals on their sheets. Kids may also wish to research and draw other extinct Ice Age mammals such as the woolly mammoth, the giant sloth, and the dire wolf.

You can extend this activity by handing out fresh copies of these pages and allowing kids to cut out the mammals and create their own museum exhibit of mammals in cave paintings by coloring and then gluing or taping each cut-out animal to a piece of poster board. Encourage kids to write a story at the bottom of their exhibit poster that explains the relationship between the cave paintings, the Ice Age mammals, and their modern cousins.

ICE AGE MAMMALS

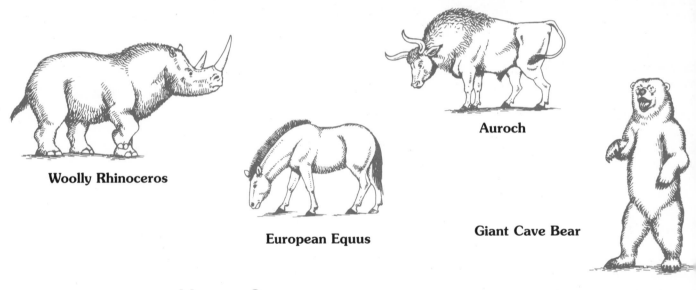

Woolly Rhinoceros

European Equus

Auroch

Giant Cave Bear

MODERN COUSINS

Dairy Cow

Appaloosa Horse

Black Bear

Black Rhino

Think Big

Compare two large mammals using models

Objectives:
Compare the skeletons of an African elephant and a right whale for similarities and differences. Research why these mammals are endangered.

Ages:
Intermediate and Advanced

Materials:
- *Copies of pages 88, 89, and 90*
- *Scissors*
- *Tape*
- *Crayons, markers*

Subjects:
Science, Art

Do your kids know what the biggest land and sea animals are? The answer is that they are mammals. Can they guess which kinds of mammals? (Answer: elephants on land and whales in the sea.)

There are only two elephant species: African and Indian. African elephants are the larger of the two. Some stand more than 12 feet (3.6 m) high and weigh over 12,000 pounds (5400 kg).

The largest whale (and the largest animal of all) is the blue whale. It can stretch about 100 feet (30 m) long and weigh 150 tons (135,000 kg). The right whale is big, too. It can grow to 60 feet (18 m) long and weigh up to 46 tons (42,000 kg).

Ask your students what they know about elephants and whales. List their responses on the board. Do they think that these huge creatures are predators like lions and tigers? If so, why? (Kids may think that only meat eaters can grow so large.) The fact is that neither the elephant, nor the blue whale, nor the right whale is such a hunter. The largest whales, in fact, are toothless. They filter tons of plankton (tiny animals, eggs, algae, and other living things that float in seawater) and small fishes from the water but do not hunt sharks, squids, and other big sea creatures. One adult elephant may eat more than 500 pounds (225 kg) of plants a day. Its ivory tusks are really long, curved teeth which can be used to peel bark from trees or as weapons against predators.

Invite kids to make the models of the African elephant standing in the grass and the right whale. (See below for instructions.) Challenge kids to compare the two skeletons. How are they alike? (Both have a backbone, ribs, a skull, etc.) How are they different? (Elephant has teeth, legs, tusks; whale has side fins, or flippers, in place of legs, baleen in place of teeth, no tusks, etc.) Explain that sheets of comblike plates, called baleen, hang from the roof of the whale's mouth. As the whale swims, it sucks in huge mouthfuls of water containing plankton. Bristles on the end of the baleen trap plankton and hold them as the whale forces the water out of its mouth. Then the whale licks the plankton off the baleen with its tongue.

Ask kids to focus on the two circles with the small bones that they attached to the sides of the whale skeleton. If the whale were a land animal, what would be where these small bones are? (Answer: legbones.) Explain that whales descended from land animals that lived millions of years ago. The small bones are what remains of the back leg bones of the whale's ancestors. The small bones are no longer even connected to the rest of the whale's skeleton.

Divide the class into two groups and challenge one group to research the elephant and the other the whale. Ask the groups to find out what is under the whale's skin that helps it keep warm in cold water, how long the whale can hold its breath, how the elephant uses its trunk, if an elephant can swim, etc. Stress that both of the animals are endangered as a result of overhunting. Have kids find out why they were hunted down and what is being down to save these mammals from extinction.

(continued next page)

MAKING THE ELEPHANT

1. Color all five elephant pieces.
2. Cut out the legs piece and fold the legs up as shown:

3. Fold in the four tabs and tape the front legs together and the back legs together as shown:

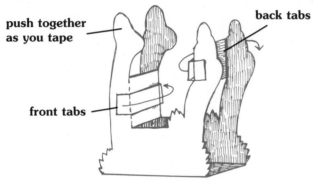

push together as you tape

front tabs

back tabs

4. Cut out the ribs and backbone piece. Fold down the middle and tape as shown.

5. Place the ribs and backbone piece on top of the legs so it hangs over the back legs. Pinch and tape the front legs together as shown.

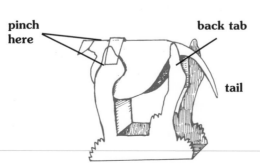

pinch here

back tab

tail

6. Cut out the skull piece and fold in half. Make a circle of tape and press the circle on the neck tab as shown. By so pressing. the other half of the tape circle will face sticky side up.

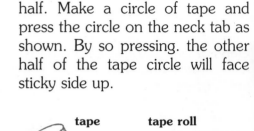

tape   tape roll

neck tab

7. Press the skull piece onto this sticky tape and pinch together as shown:

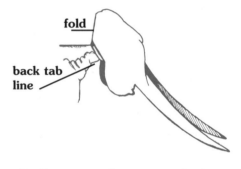

fold

back tab line

8. Cut out the two elephant side pieces and tape together as shown. Then place the outside of the elephant over the skeleton.

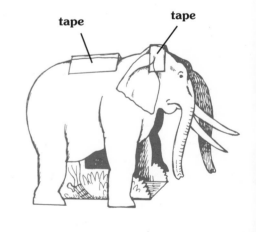

tape   tape

MAKING THE WHALE

1. Color the seven whale pieces.
2. Cut out the ribs and backbone piece, fold in half and tape as shown:

3. Cut out the right flipper bones and tape to the right side of the ribs using the white line as a guide. Cut out the right circle and tape in place as shown.

angle leg back

hind limb

4. Repeat for the left flipper bones and left circle.
5. Cut out the skull piece making sure to cut around the white triangle. Fold the piece in half and fold the triangle flap as shown:

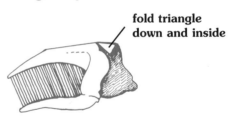

fold triangle down and inside

6. Make a circle of tape and press half of it on the front end of the ribs and backbone piece as shown. The other half of the circle will face sticky side up.

tape roll

neck tab

7. Press the skull on top of the sticky tape using the folded triangle as a guide as shown:

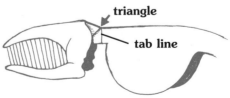

triangle

tab line

8. Cut out the outside of the whale making sure to cut out the inner area labeled WHALE. Fold this piece in half and place over the whale skeleton as shown:

skelton inside

THAT'S A MOUTHFUL!

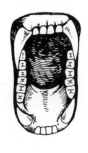

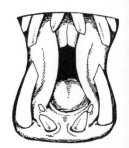

Two mazes to try.

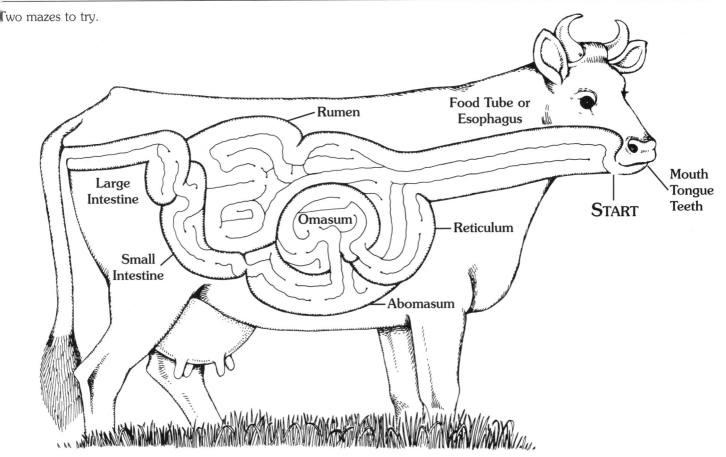

Rumen

Food Tube or Esophagus

Large Intestine

Omasum

Reticulum

Mouth
Tongue
Teeth

START

Small Intestine

Abomasum

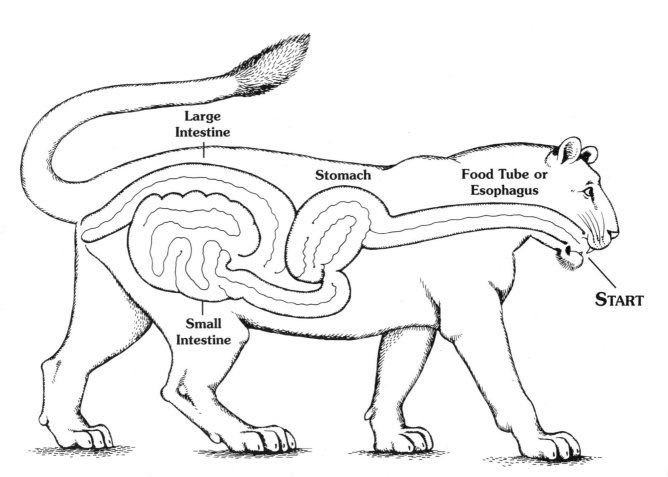

Large Intestine

Stomach

Food Tube or Esophagus

Small Intestine

START

30,000 YEAR OLD CAVE PAINTING, FRANCE

ICE AGE MAMMALS

MODERN COUSINS

Mountain Gorilla

Timber Wolf

Black Rhinoceros

Steller's Sea Lion

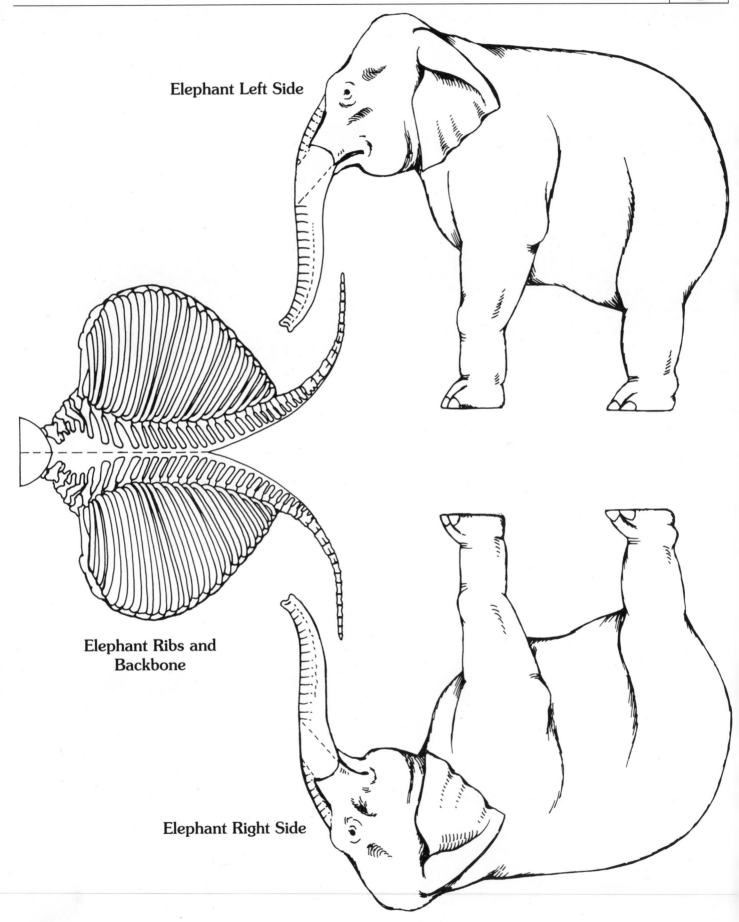

Elephant Left Side

Elephant Ribs and
Backbone

Elephant Right Side

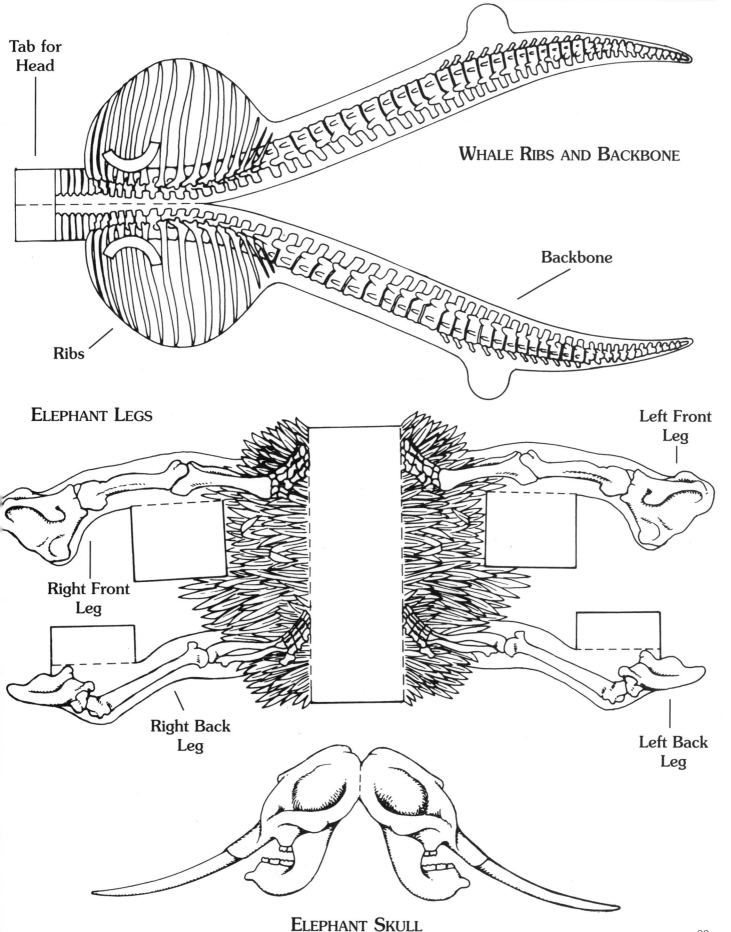

Tab for
Head

WHALE RIBS AND BACKBONE

Backbone

Ribs

ELEPHANT LEGS

Left Front
Leg

Right Front
Leg

Right Back
Leg

Left Back
Leg

ELEPHANT SKULL

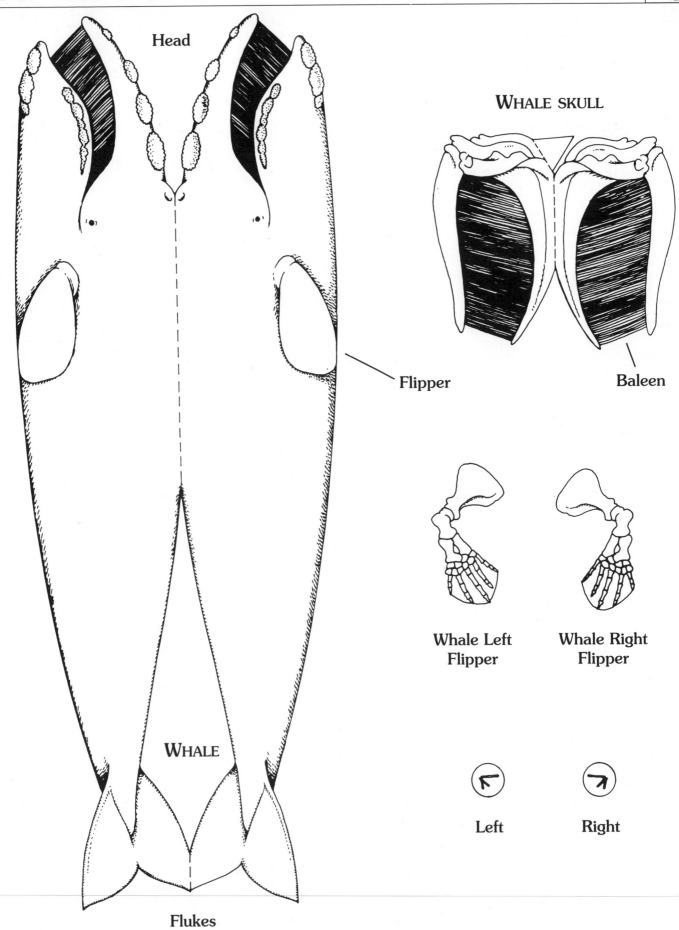

Head

WHALE SKULL

Flipper

Baleen

Whale Left
Flipper

Whale Right
Flipper

WHALE

Left

Right

Flukes

Bibliography

(Note: A * at the end of a listing indicates that a book is a good source of mammal pictures.)

GENERAL REFERENCE BOOKS

The Encyclopedia of Mammals edited by Dr. David Macdonald (Facts on File, 1984). *

Handbook to the Orders and Families of Living Mammals by Timothy E. Lawlor (Mad River Press, 1979).

Walker's Mammals of the World, 5th edition, edited by Ronald M. Nowak (John Hopkins University Press, 1991). Two volumes *

Warm-blooded Animals by Maurice Burton (Facts on File, 1985). *

Wild Animals of North America edited by Thomas P. Allen (National Geographic, 1979). Item #A101958 *

Wildlife Alert! The Struggle to Survive by Gene S. Stuart (National Geographic, 1980).

FIELD GUIDES

The Audubon Society Field Guide to North American Mammals by John O. Whitaker, Jr. (Knopf, 1996). *

A Field Guide to Animal Tracks by Olaus J. Murie (Houghton Mifflin, 1974).

A Field Guide to the Mammals by William Henry Burt and Richard P. Grossenheider (Houghton Mifflin, 1976). *

Identifying Animal Tracks by Richard Headstrom (Dover Publications, 1983).

Mammals by Herbert Zim and Donald Hoffmeister (Western Publishing Co., 1987). *

Mammals of North America by John A. Burton and Angela Royston, a Science Nature Guide, (Thunder Bay Press, 1995). *

Simon and Schuster's Guide to Mammals edited by Sydney Anderson (Simon and Schuster, 1984). *

Tom Brown's Field Guide to Nature Observation and Tracking by Tom Brown and Morgan Brandt (Berkley Books, 1986). *

CHILDREN'S BOOKS

101 Questions & Answers about Backyard Wildlife by Ann Squire (Walker, 1996). Primary and Intermediate

A Bold Carnivore: An Alphabet of Predators by Consie Powell (Roberts Rinehart, 1995). Primary

A is for Arctic: Natural Wonders of a Polar World by Wayne Lynch (Firefly Books, 1996). Advanced *

About Mammals by Cathryn P. Sill (Peachtree Publishers Ltd., 1997). Primary

African Animals by Caroline Arnold (Morrow, 1997). Primary *

America's Deserts: Guide to Plants and Animals by Marianne Wallace (Fulcrum Publishing, 1996). Primary and Intermediate

Animal Babies by Claire Craig, from the Nature Company Young Discoveries Library, (Time-Life Books, 1996). Primary

Animal Dads by Sneed B. Collard (Houghton Mifflin, 1997). Primary

Animal Homes by Barbara Taylor (Dorling Kindersley, 1996). Intermediate

Animal Senses by Melvin Berger, part of the Ranger Rick's® Science Spectacular Series, (Newbridge Communications, 1995). Primary *

Animals in Danger by Melvin Berger, part of the Ranger Rick's® Science Spectacular Series, (Newbridge Communications, 1993). Primary *

Animals in Winter by Henrietta Bancroft and Richard Van Gelder, part of the Let's-Read-and-Find-Out Science Series, (HarperCollins, 1997). Primary

Animals in Winter (National Geographic, 1996). Primary and Intermediate

Arctic Babies by Kathy Darling (Walker, 1996). Primary and Intermediate *

Baby Animals by Richard Roe (Random House, 1985). Primary

Big, Rough, and Wrinkly by Moira Butterfield (Raintree Steck-Vaughn, 1997). Primary

Brown, Fierce, and Furry by Moira Butterfield (Raintree Steck-Vaughn, 1997). Primary

City Kids and City Critters by Janet Wier Roberts and Carole Huelbig (McGraw-Hill, 1998).

Crinkleroot's Guide to Knowing Animal Habitats (Simon and Schuster, 1997). Primary

Desert Babies by Kathy Darling (Walker, 1997). Primary *

Desert Mammals by Elaine Landau, part of the A True Book series, (Children's Press, 1996). Primary *

Endangered Animals by Gallimard Jeunesse and Sylvaine Perols, A First Discovery Book, (Scholastic Inc., 1997). Primary

Endangered Animals by Lynn M. Stone (Children's Press, 1984). Primary

Extraordinary Animals: Baby Animals by Andrew Brown (Crabtree Publishing Co., 1997). Primary

Extraordinary Animals: Dangerous Animals by Andrew Brown (Crabtree Publishing Co., 1997). Primary

Extremely Weird Mammals by Sarah Lovett (John Muir Publications, 1993). Primary *

Eyewitness Books: Mammal by Steven Parker (Knopf, 1989). Intermediate and Advanced

Eyewitness Explorers: Mammals by David Burnie (Dorling Kindersley, 1993). Intermediate

Eyewitness Juniors 2: Amazing Mammals by Alexandra Parsons (Knopf, 1990). Intermediate and Advanced

Giants from the Past (National Geographic, 1983). Intermediate and Advanced *

Grassland Mammals by Elaine Landau, part of the A True Book series, (Children's Press, 1996). Primary *

How Animals Communicate by Bobbie Kalman (Crabtree Publishing Co., 1996). Primary

How Do Animals Sleep? by Melvin Berger, part of the Ranger Rick's® Science Spectacular Series, (Newbridge Communications, 1996). Primary *

Kenneth Lilly's Animals by Kenneth Lilly with text by Joyce Pope. (Walker Books Ltd., 1988). Primary and Intermediate

The Kingfisher Illustrated Encyclopedia of Animals consulting editor Michael Chinery (Kingfisher Books, 1992). Intermediate and Advanced

Kratts' Creatures: Creatures in Crisis by Chris Kratt and Martin Kratt (Scholastic Inc., 1997). Primary *

Kratts' Creatures: Our Favorite Creatures by Chris Kratt and Martin Kratt (Scholastic Inc., 1997). Primary

Life in the Desert by Melvin Berger, part of the Ranger Rick's® Science Spectacular Series, (Newbridge Communications, 1996). Primary *

Life in the Polar Regions by Melvin Berger, part of the Ranger Rick's® Science Spectacular Series, (Newbridge Communications, 1994). Primary *

Life in the Rainforest by Melvin Berger, part of the Ranger Rick's® Science Spectacular Series, (Newbridge Communications, 1993). Primary *

Life in Your Backyard by Natalie Lunis, part of the Ranger Rick's® Science Spectacular Series, (Newbridge Communications, 1996). Primary *

Life on the African Savannah by Melvin Berger, part of the Ranger Rick's® Science Spectacular Series, (Newbridge Communications, 1995). Primary *

MacMillan Children's Guide to Endangered Animals by Roger Few (MacMillan Publishing, 1993). Intermediate

Mammals part of the Nature Library Reptiles and Amphibians series (National Geographic, 1993). Primary and Intermediate *

Mammals by Gallimard Jeunesse, part of the Scholastic Voyages of Discovery Natural History series, (Scholastic Inc., 1997). Intermediate

Mammals consulting editor Dr. George McKay, part of The Nature Company Discoveries Series Library, (Weldon Owen Pty Ltd., 1996). Intermediate

The Mighty Ocean by Melvin Berger, part of the Ranger Rick's® Science Spectacular Series, (Newbridge Communications, 1996). Primary *

Mountain Mammals by Elaine Landau, part of the A True Book series, (Children's Press, 1996). Primary *

Nature in Danger: Threatened Habitats and Species by Noel Simon (Oxford University, 1995). Advanced

Nature's World Records. by John R. Quinn (McGraw-Hill, 1996).

One Small Square: African Savanna by Donald M. Silver, illustrated by Patricia J. Wynne (McGraw-Hill, 1997).

One Small Square: Back Yard by Donald M. Silver, illustrated by Patricia J. Wynne (McGraw-Hill, 1997).

Polar Mammals by Larry Dane Brimner, part of the A True Book series, (Children's Press, 1996). Primary *

Powerful Beasts of the Wild by Theresa Greenaway (Dorling Kindersley, 1997). Primary and Intermediate

Prehistoric Mammals by Anne McCord (Usborne, 1977). Intermediate and Advanced

Rain Forest Babies by Kathy Darling (Walker, 1996). Primary and Intermediate *

Small Mammals Are Where You Find Them by Helen Tee-Van (Knopf, 1967). Primary and Intermediate

Spin's Really Wild U.S.A. Tour by Barbara Brownell (National Geographic, 1996). Primary *

Temperate Forest Mammals by Elaine Landau, part of the A True Book series, (Children's Press, 1996). Primary *

Tropical Forest Mammals by Elaine Landau, part of the A True Book series, (Children's Press, 1996). Primary *

Walk on the Wild Side! by Connie and Peter Roop (Millbrook, 1997). Primary and Intermediate

Why Do Animals Do That? by Bobbie Kalman (Crabtree Publishing Co., 1996). Primary

Wild Animals of North America (National Geographic, 1995) Primary, Intermediate and Advanced

Wild Babies by Seymour Simon (HarperCollins, 1997). Primary and Intermediate *

Zoobooks (Wildlife Education Ltd.) Published in periodical form, and available in many libraries and specialty gift shops. To order write to Zoobooks, 9820 Willow Creek Road, Suite 300, San Diego CA 92131 or call 1-800-477-5034. For subscriptions call 1-800-992-5034. *

CD-ROM & COMPUTER SOFTWARE

ABC World Reference: Wide World of Animals CD-ROM by Creative Wonders, 1996. To order write Electronic Arts, Box 7530, San Mateo CA 94403 or call 1-800-543-9778. (Intermediate and Advanced)

Amazing Animals CD-ROM Activity Pack by Dorling Kindersley, 1997. Includes an Amazing Animals video. (Primary)

Animal Planet CD-ROM by The Discovery Channel, 1996. To order call 1-800-762-2189. (Intermediate)

Animals and How They Grow Mac/Windows software program part of the Wonders of Learning Library. National Geographic, 1994. To order call National Geographic 1-800-368-2728. (Primary)

DK Eyewitness Children's Encyclopedia CD-ROM by Dorling Kindersley, 1997. (Primary and Intermediate)

Encyclopedia of U.S. Endangered Species CD-ROM by ZCI publishing, 1995. (Intermediate)

Exploring Animal Life CD-ROM. To order write CLEARVUE-eav, 6465 North Avondale Avenue, Chicago IL 60631 or call 1-800-253-2788. Orders can be faxed to 1-800-444-9855. (Intermediate and Advanced)

The Five Kingdoms of Life CD-ROM. To order contact CLEARVUE-eav, 6465 North Avondale Avenue, Chicago IL 60631 or call 1-800-253-2788. Orders can be faxed to 1-800-444-9855. (Intermediate)

Learning All About Animals CD-ROM. To order contact CLEARVUE-eav, 6465 North Avondale Avenue, Chicago IL 60631 or call 1-800-253-2788. Orders can be faxed to 1-800-444-9855. (Intermediate and Advanced)

Mammals: A Multimedia Encyclopedia CD-ROM by National Geographic, 1990. (Primary, Intermediate and Advanced)

Multimedia Animals Encyclopedia CD-ROM. To order contact SVE & Churchill Media 6677 N. Northwest Highway, Chicago IL 60631 or call 1-800-829-1900. Orders may be faxed to 1-800-624-1678. (Intermediate and Advanced)

My First Encyclopedia CD-ROM by Knowledge Adventure, 1994. To order call 1-800-542-4240. (Primary)

STV: Animals an interactive video disc by National Geographic, 1993. (Primary)

The Random House Kids Encyclopedia CD-ROM by Knowledge Adventure, 1994. To order call 1-800-542-4240. (Primary and Intermediate)

Undersea Adventure CD-ROM by Knowledge Adventure, 1994. To order call 1-800-542- 4240. (Primary and Intermediate)

Vertebrates: Mammals and **Mammals 2** CD-ROM. To order contact SVE & Churchill Media 6677 N. Northwest Highway, Chicago IL 60631 or call 1-800-829-1900. Orders may be faxed to 1-800-624-1678. (Intermediate and Advanced)

Whales And Dolphins: Zooguides CD-ROM by REMedia/Sony Electronic Publishing, 1994. (Intermediate)

Wild Africa: Ngorongoro, Serengeti, Tarangire CD-ROM. To order contact SVE & Churchill Media 6677 N. Northwest Highway, Chicago IL 60631 or call 1-800-829-1900. Orders may be faxed to 1-800-624-1678. (Intermediate and Advanced)

The World of Nature CD-ROM by Queue Inc., 1995. To order write Queue Inc. 338 Commerce Drive, Fairfield CT 06432 or call 1-800-232-2224. (Intermediate)

FILMS, FILMSTRIPS, SLIDE SETS AND VIDEOS

Adaptation for Survival: Mammals (Intermediate and Advanced) and **Living Mammal** (Intermediate and Advanced) are available in video. Order from International Film Bureau, Inc., 322 S. Michigan Avenue, Chicago IL 60604.

African Animal Safari: Animals of the Plains (Primary) video includes teacher's guide. Produced by Churchill Video Ventures, 1995.

The Age of Mammals (Primary, Intermediate and Advanced) is an animated film on prehistoric mammals, and **Mammals** (Primary) is a musical film on characteristics. To order write AIMS Media, 9710 DeSoto Avenue, Chatsworth CA 91311 or call 1-800-367-2467. Orders may be faxed to 1-818-341-6700.

Amazing Animals (Primary) video series. Titles include Animal Journeys, Animal Senses, Animal Survivors, Armored Animals, Mini-Beasts, Poisonous Animals, Nighttime Animals and Animal Appetites. Distributed by DK Publishing.

Animal Classes: Mammals (Intermediate). This unusual video was created by a middle school student who put together video clips, graphics, animations, stills and cartoons that demonstrate Lashawn's research into what makes an animal a mammal. National Geographic, 1996.

Animals and How They Grow: Mammals (Primary) filmstrip discusses how young animals grow and change. National Geographic, 1993. To order call 1-800-368-2728.

Carolina Biological Supply has slide sets on many mammal topics including horns and antlers, endangered species and mammal predators. Each set comes with a printed guide. For more information write Carolina Biological Supply

Company, 2700 York Road, Burlington NC 27215 or call 1-800-334-5551.

Catch Me If You Can: The Predators & The Grazers (Primary, Intermediate and Advanced) This video teaches children about animal behavior and its importance for animal survival. Produced by Bob Landis, Landis Wildlife Films.

Mammal Slide Library is sponsored by the American Society of Mammalogists and offers 900 different color slides of over 600 mammal species. For more information, write Elmer Finck, American Mammalogists Society Slide Library, Emporia State University, 1200 Commercial, Box 4050, Emporia KS 66801.

Marine Mammals (Intermediate) from the "Bill Nye, the Science Guy" television series. Disney Educational Productions, 1996. To order contact Disney Educational Productions 501 S. Cherry, Suite 350, Denver CO 80222

North American Animals and ***Animals Around the World*** (Primary) are filmstrips which discuss how human carelessness threatens animals in North America and around the world. By National Geographic, 1994. To order call 1-800-368-2728.

See How They Grow: Wild Animals (Rabbits, Foxes, Pheasants, Snakes) (Intermediate) This video features fun, fascinating and factual information on how animals grow up. To order call Environmental Media at 1-800-368-3382.

The Structure of Animals Filmstrip Series. Part 2 covers Vertebrates (Intermediate and Advanced) by National Geographic, 1987. To order call 1-800-368-2728.

Where Do Animals Go in Winter? (Primary) video discusses how animals adjust to the cold and scarcity of food during the winter by National Geographic, 1995. To order call 1-800-368-2728.

Who Lives Here? Filmstrip Series. (Primary) Part I covers *Animals in Backyards* and *Animals In and Around Ponds* and Part 2 covers *Animals of the Sea* and *Animals in the Desert* by National Geographic, 1990. To order call 1-800-368-2728.

Wild, Wonderful Animals in the Woods (Primary) part of The Unlovables video series by National Geographic, 1996. To order call 1-800-368-2728.

Zoo Food with Grandpa Nature (Primary) video by Milestone Media, 1996 and distributed by 411 Video Information.

BOOKLETS, KITS, MAPS

The Curious Naturalist, (Massachusetts Audubon Society, 1995). To order write Massachusetts Audubon Society, Educational Resources Office, 208 South Great Road, Lincoln MA 01773 or call 1-617-259-9500 x7255.

An Educational Coloring Book of Mammals edited by Linda Spizzirri (Spizzirri Publishing Co., 1981).

An Educational Coloring Book of Prehistoric Mammals edited by Linda Spizzirri (Spizzirri Publishing Co., 1981).

Eye on the Environment: Wildlife Poster Set from National Geographic Society includes three posters and a teacher's guide. National Geographic, 1995. (Primary, Intermediate and Advanced)

Mammals and How They Grow (Primary) is a *Wonders of Learning Kit* by the National Geographic Society, 1984. The kit contains a cassette and read-along booklets for 25, ready-to-copy activity sheets and teacher's guide. For a catalog write to National Geographic, PO Box 11650, Des Moines IA 50340. Or call 1-888-647-6733 to place your order.

Upclose Kits include *Desert Wildlife, Polar Wildlife, Forest Wildlife* and *Ocean Wildlife*. By Joshua Morris from Reader's Digest Association Inc.

U.S. Government Printing Office has posters and publications on many mammal subjects. To order list of items write Superintendent of Documents, U.S. Government Printing Office, PO Box 371954, Pittsburgh PA 15250-7954.

Whales (Primary) is a *Wonders of Learning Kit* by the National Geographic, 1984. To order call 1-800-368-2728.

OTHER ACTIVITY SOURCES

Hands on Nature: Information and Activities for Exploring the Environment with Children (Vermont Institute of Natural Science, 1986). Mammal-related activities include "Meet a Deer," "Rabbits and Foxes," and "Snug in Snow." To order write to Whitman Distribution Center, 10 Water Street, Lebanon NH 03766 or call 1-603-448-0037.

Project WILD, developed by the Council for Environmental Education. To order write Project WILD, 5430 Grosvenor Lane, Suite 230, Bethesda MD 20814 or call 1-301-493-5447. Visit their web site at http://eelink.umich.edu/wild/

WHERE TO GET MORE INFORMATION

• National Wildlife Federation's (NWF) Conservation Directory
• NWF's *Conservation Directory* is the most comprehensive listing of environmental conservation organizations. Each easy-to-read entry contains all the information you need: names, addresses, telephone/fax numbers and description of program areas. The *Conservation Directory* is a valuable resource tool for people active in the field, students and adults looking for further information on various animal and plant species, and those seeking employment in natural resource management and conservation careers.
• If you want to know the who, what, and where about environmental organizations, this is the book for you. The *Conservation Directory* can be ordered by writing to the National Wildlife Federation, 8925 Leesburg Pike, Vienna VA 22184. For discount pricing contact Rue Gordon at 703-790-4402.
• College and university departments of biology, mammalogy or zoology
• Museums
• Zoos
• Nature centers
• World Wide Web sites:
National Wildlife Federation http://www.nwf.org
U.S. Fish and Wildlife Service http://www.fws.gov
U.S. Fish and Wildlife Service-Wildlife Species Fact Sheets http://www.fws.gov/~r9extaff/biologues/wildspp.html
Project WILD http://eelink.umich.edu/wild/
The Electronic Zoo http://netuet/wustl.edu/e-zoo.htm
IWC (International Wildlife Coalition) http://www.webcom/wcwww/teachers_kit/learn.html
World Wildlife Fund fact sheets http://www.panda.org/research/factSheets/BrownBear/index.htm
EE-Link Endangered Species information http://eelink.umich.edu/EndSpp/Endangered.html
Omnibus K-12 Science Server http://www.pen.k12.va.us/Anthology/Div/Charlottesville/SCHOOLS/CHS/RESOURCES

Internet Address Disclaimer:

The Internet information provided here was correct, to the best of our knowledge, at the time of publication. It is important to remember, however, the dynamic nature of the Internet. Resources that are free and publicly available one day may require a fee or restrict access the next, and the location of items may change as menus and homepages are reorganized.

Natural Resources

Ranger Rick, *published by the National Wildlife Federation, is a monthly nature magazine for elementary-age children.*

Ranger Rick*®** magazine is an excellent source of additional information and activities on dinosaurs and many other aspects of nature, outdoor adventure, and the environment. This 48-page award-winning monthly publication of the National Wildlife Federa-tion is packed with the highest-quality color photos, illustrations, and both fiction and nonfiction articles. All factual information in ***Ranger Rick has been checked for accuracy by experts in the field. The articles, games, puzzles, photo-stories, crafts, and other features inform as well as entertain and can easily be adapted for classroom use. To order or for more information, call 1-800-588-1650.

The EarthSavers Club provides an excellent opportunity for you and your students to join thousands of others across the country in helping to improve our environment. Sponsored by Target Stores and the National Wildlife Federation, this program provides children aged 6 to 14 and their adult leaders with free copies of the award-winning ***EarthSavers*** newspaper and ***Activity Guide*** four times during the school year, along with a leader's handbook, EarthSavers Club certificate, and membership cards. For more information on how to join, call 1-703-790-4535 or write to EarthSavers; National Wildlife Federation; 8925 Leesburg Pike; Vienna, VA 22184.

Index